أوراد الشيخ الأكبر
محيي الدين ابن العربي

Litanies of the Greatest Master
Muḥyīddīn Ibn al-ʿArabī

Compiled and Translated by

Dr. Ali Hussain

Foreword by

Imam Adeyinka Muhammad Mendes

I0389282

First Edition December 2022

ISBN: 978-1-938058-67-7

Printed in the United States of America.

Library of Congress Cataloging-in-Publication Data

TBD

Published and Distributed by:

Institute for Spiritual and Cultural Advancement

17195 Silver Parkway, #401
Fenton, MI 48430 USA
Tel: (888) 278-6624
Fax:(810) 815-0518
Email: info@sufilive.com
Web: http://www.sufilive.com
Photo Credit: Joel Vodell on Unsplash

Table of Contents

Foreword i

Introduction vii

The Prophetic Benediction of the Essence 1

The Greatest Prophetic Benediction of Unfolding 3

The Litany of Protection for the One Desiring Sainthood 23

Litanies for Days of the Week 41

- The Night of Sunday 43
- The Day of Sunday 49
- The Night of Monday 67
- The Day of Monday 75
- The Night of Tuesday 85
- The Day of Tuesday 91
- The Night of Wednesday 97
- The Day of Wednesday 105
- The Night of Thursday 109
- The Day of Thursday 115
- The Night of Friday 131
- The Day of Friday 139
- The Night of Saturday 145
- The Day of Saturday 153

بِسْمِ اللَّهِ الرَّحْمَٰنِ الرَّحِيمِ

Foreword

All praise and thanks are due to the Absolute Reality Who made Islam (loving surrender) a Living Path of tradition, transmission, transaction, transformation, and transcendence.

May our Beloved Creator always exalt, bless, and grant peace to Muhammad ﷺ the Universal Prophet who was sent as a gift of God's Love to all nations and beings, along with his immaculate family and noble companions who were vessels of divine knowledge and compassionate care for creation.

And all the Prophets, Messengers, guides, and sages sent by Absolute Reality to teach human beings the highest goals for our existence: experiential knowledge of God's Presence, loving embodiment of Prophet Muhammad's ﷺ sublime character (divine peace and blessings on him), and selflessly benefitting our fellow creatures with our individual gifts.

Shaykh Muḥyīddīn Ibn al-ʿArabī (God have mercy on his soul), affectionally known by those who value his vast spiritual and intellectual legacy as the Greatest Spiritual Master (*al-Shaykh al-Akbar*), is among the most effective and influential sages, guides, and teachers sent to humanity to transmit and explain the five dimensions of a holistic and healing Islam: law (*sharīʿa*), spiritual journeying (*ṭarīqa*), metaphysical reality (*ḥaqīqa*), divine knowledge (*maʿrifa*), and Absolute Truth (*ḥaqq*).

These are all summed up in the virtues of faith (*īmān*), loving surrender (*islām*) and inner excellence (*iḥsān*). It is the awareness and appreciation of these five dimensions that was the secret to the greatness of Muslim cultures and civilizations from the Mali Empire to the Malay Archipelago in the pre-colonial era.

Their arts and sciences continue to inspire and benefit the whole world regardless of their culture or religion. It has been the disconnection and severance of

Muslims from these five dimensions that has resulted in a Muslim community that struggles to provide centeredness, healing, and balance to people in our very imbalanced brave new modern and post-modern worlds.

Many of us share a collective amnesia of Shaykh Ibn al-ʿArabī's incredible contributions to human wisdom. My dear friend, Dr. Ali Hussain, has translated and transliterated, from Arabic to English, one such contribution to remind us of our greatest potential as human beings. To awaken us from our global sleep so that we may restore equilibrium to our hearts, our homes, and our planet.

The supplications and litanies of Shaykh Ibn al-ʿArabī are not only poetically beautiful, but they also have a transformative power. These prayers have been a means to healing, enlightenment, and divine empowerment for thousands of seekers for hundreds of years. For the first time in almost a millennium the prayers before you have been allowed to breathe in the

English language by a respected scholar of the works of Shaykh Ibn al-ʿArabī who strives to engage and experience those works, not reduce them to mere objects of academic study.

In this spirit, Dr. Hussain has presented not just any supplication of Shaykh Ibn al-ʿArabī. Rather, he has carefully curated a collection of Prayers Upon the Prophet Muhammad ﷺ (divine peace and blessings upon him). Muslim scholars and sages agree that asking the Creator to bestow blessings and peace on the Prophet Muhammed ﷺ (divine peace and blessings on him) is among the greatest means to receive God's material bounties, mercy, grace, guidance, healing, joy, and love.

It is a prayer that is always answered, an act that God and His angels are always doing, and a means to strengthen one's connection with the person, spirit, and primordial light of the Prophet Muhammad ﷺ (divine peace and blessings on him) as well as those of other prophets, messengers, sages, and spiritual teachers sent by God.

We are in indebted to Dr. Hussain for producing a translation of these litanies from Shaykh Ibn al-ʿArabī that is readable, beautiful, powerful, and full of practical wisdom, as well as spiritual mysteries that only those who have divinely enlightened hearts comprehend.

These prayers are an exquisite tapestry of the five dimensions of Islam in an attractive and accessible form. May Allah, our Beloved Creator, make this book a means of material prosperity, moral edification, character refinement, community development, and spiritual elevation for all who own it, read it, memorize it, glance at it, and encourage others towards it.

We ask Allah to make this happen through the Power of His Beautiful Names, and the sanctity of our beloved healer, emancipator, teacher, and Prophet

Muhammad ﷺ (divine peace and blessings on him, his wives, family, companions, and descendants).

Amen.

Adeyinka Muhammad Mendes

Medina, Saudi Arabia

December 3, 2022 (Jumādā ath-Thānya 9, 1444)

بِسْمِ اللهِ الرَّحْمٰنِ الرَّحِيمِ

Introduction

"You have to be a poet to understand Ibn al-ʿArabī"

- Mawlana Shaykh Hisham Kabbani

"For every age, there is one to ennoble it,
and I am, for that age, this one"

- Shaykh al-Akbar Muḥyīddīn Ibn al-ʿArabī

All praise is due to Allah ﷻ who facilitates for His servants to love Him, only because He loved them first. The height of that love manifests in prophets and messengers, most auspiciously in their master and leader, our beloved Muhammad ﷺ, his family, companions and those who follow them in guidance until the end of time.

Thenceforth, those who inherit that love and light from *sayyidi-l-wujūd* (the master of existence) ﷺ, his family and companions, become known as *awliyāʾ* (saints/friends of God), the pegs and mountains who carry divine secrets and serve as trustees over His creation. He gazes through them at the universe, and they are ʿUyūnu-l-Raḥmān (The Eyes of the Most-Merciful).

From among them, still few are chosen as *aqṭāb* (poles), or even a *ghawth* (succor) for creation, that singular representative who answers directly to our master Muhammad ﷺ and carries out his wishes for *ummatu-l-daʿwah* (entire creation) and *ummatu-l-ijābah* (community of believing Muslims).

Across the generations, since the beginning of Islam through the blessed birth of *sayyidu-l-wujūd* ﷺ, there have been many such unique singularities: Sidi ʿAbdul Qādir al-Jīlānī, Imām Abū Ḥāmid al-Ghazālī and, the heart of this book, al-Shaykh al-Akbar Muḥyīddīn Ibn al-ʿArabī.

This book represents a humble attempt by a lover of the *awliyāʾ* and Shaykh al-Akbar specifically to express his love for his guide(s), by compiling, transliterating, and translating the celestial litanies of *khatm al-walāya al-muḥammadiyyah* (the seal of Muhammadan sainthood), a lofty spiritual rank that was granted to Shaykh al-Akbar during his life.

There have been many printed editions of the litanies found in this book, in the original Arabic, but none so far rendered in English, much less transliterated. I have used, as reference, many of these Arabic editions in my attempt and, therefore, the version you find here is a newly collated critical edition, so to say.

To the utmost of my ability, I have tried explaining key terms in the Shaykh's writings and some of my translation choices in the footnotes. To fully appreciate the power and potency of these litanies, the reader must be consistent in reciting them daily, filling one's heart with love for the Shaykh, the Beloved ﷺ and Allah Almighty ﷻ.

I ask Allah ﷻ to grant us a gaze from Shaykh al-Akbar, that He makes this humble book a means for us to be gathered with the Shaykh and our guides in this life and the hereafter and a window to obtain His contentment and love until eternity and beyond.

وآخِرُ دَعْوَانَا أَنْ الحَمْدُ لله رَبِّ العَالَمِينْ

وَ مَا تَوْفِيقِي إِلَّا بالله

بِسْمِ اللهِ الرَّحْمٰنِ الرَّحِيمِ

Bismillāh ar-Raḥmān ar-Raḥīm

In the Name of Allah,

Most-Beneficent, Most Merciful

الحَمْدُ لله رَبِّ العَالَمِينَ

وَالصَّلاةُ وَالسَّلامُ عَلَى سَيِّدِنَا مُحَمَّدٍ وَعَلى آلِهِ وَصَحْبِهِ أَجْمَعِينْ

Al-ḥamdu lillāhi Rabbil ʿĀlamīn wa-ṣ-ṣalātu wa-s-salāmu ʿalā sayyidinā Muḥammadin wa ʿalā ālihi wa ṣahbihi ajmaʿīn

All Praise is due to Allah, the Lord of the Worlds. Immense Prayers and Salutations upon our Master Muhammad ﷺ, his family and companions in their entirety.

الصَّلاة الذَّاتِيَّة

Aṣ-Ṣalāt a-dh-dhātiyyah[1]

The Prophetic Benediction of the Essence

اَللَّهُمَّ صَلِّ عَلَى الْذَّاتِ الْمُطَلْسَمِ وَالْغَيْبِ الْمُطَمْطَمِ

Allāhumma ṣalli ʿalā-dh-dhāti-l-muṭalsami wa-l-ghaybi-l-muṭamṭam

Oh Allah, send prayers upon the enigmatic essence and overflowing unseen

[1] There are many variations for this ṣalawāt. Mawlana Shaykh Hisham Kabbani, Allah preserve him, has given this formula.

لَاهُوتِ الْجَمَالِ نَاسُوتِ الْوِصَالِ

lāhūti-l-jamāl nāsūti-l-wiṣāl
The principles of Divine Beauty
and human intimacy

طَلْعَةِ الْحَقِّ كَنْزِ عَيْنِ إِنْسَانِ الْأَزَلِ فِي نَشْرِ مَنْ لَمْ يَزَلْ

ṭalʿati-l-ḥaqqi kanzi ʿayni insāni-l-azali fī nashri man lam yazal
The emergence of the Truth, treasure of the essence of the pre-eternal human in dispersion of what remains

فِي قَابِ نَاسُوتِ الْوِصَالِ الْأَقْرَبِ

fī qābi nāsūti-l-wiṣāli-l-aqrab
In the distance of the nearest portion of human intimacy

اَللَّهُمَّ صَلِّ بِهِ مِنْهُ فِيهِ عَلَيْهِ وَسَلِّم

Allāhumma ṣalli bihi minhu fīhi ʿalayhi wa sallim
Oh Allah, send prayers through, from, within and upon him with abundant peace.

بِسۡمِ ٱللَّهِ ٱلرَّحۡمَٰنِ ٱلرَّحِيمِ

Bismillāh ar-Raḥmān ar-Raḥīm

In the Name of Allah, Most-Beneficent, Most Merciful

الحَمْدُ لله رَبِّ العَالَمِينَ

وَالصَّلاةُ وَالسَّلامُ عَلَى سَيِّدِنَا مُحَمَّدٍ وَعَلى آلِهِ وَصَحْبِهِ أَجْمَعِينْ

Al-ḥamdu lillāhi Rabbil ʿĀlamīn wa-ṣ-ṣalātu wa-s-salāmu ʿalā sayyidinā Muḥammadin wa ʿalā ālihi wa ṣahbihi ajmaʿīn

All Praise is due to Allah, the Lord of the Worlds. Immense Prayers and Salutations upon our Master Muhammad ﷺ, his family and companions in their entirety.

الصَّلاةُ الفَيْضِيَّةُ الكُبْرَى

Aṣ-Ṣalāt al-Fayḍiyya al-Kubrā

The Greatest Prophetic Benediction of Unfolding

اللهُمَّ أَفِضْ صِلَةَ صَلَوَاتِكَ وَسَلَامَةَ تَسْلِيمَاتِكَ

Allāhumma afiḍ ṣilata ṣalawātika wa salāmata taslīmātika

Oh Allah, unfold the Intimacy of Your Prayers and Peace of Your Salutations

عَلَى أَوَّلِ التَّعَيُّنَاتِ المُفَاضَةِ مِنَ العَمَاءِ الرَّبَّانِي

ʿalā awwali-t-taʿayyunāt al-mufāḍati min-al-ʿamāʾi-r-Rabbānī

Upon the first of entities overflowing from the Lordly Cloud

وَآخِرِ التَنَزُّلَاتِ الْمُضَافَةِ إِلى النَوْعِ الإِنْسَانِي

wa ākhiri-t-tanazzulāti-l-muḍāfati ilā-n-nawʿil-insānī

And he who is the final descent, added to the human species

الْمُهَاجِرِ مِنْ مَكَّةَ "كَانَ اللهُ وَلَمْ يَكُنْ مَعَهُ شَيْءٍ ثَانٍ"

al-muhājiri min Makkata
"Kāna Allāhu wa lam yakun maʿahu shayʾun thānin"

He who migrates from the Mecca of
"Allah was and no second thing was with Him"

إِلى مَدِينَةِ "وَهُوَ الآنَ عَلَى مَا عَلَيْهِ كَانْ"

ilā Madīnati "Wa huwa-l-āna ʿalā mā ʿalayhi kān"

To the Madina of "And He is now as He has always been"

مُحْصِي عَوَالِمَ الحَضَرَاتِ الإِلَهِيَّةِ الخَمْسِ فِي وُجُودِهِ "وَكُلَّ شَيْءٍ أَحْصَيْنَاهُ فِي إِمَامٍ مُبِينْ"

muḥsī ʿawālima-l-ḥaḍarāti-l-ilāhiyyati-l-khamsi fī wujūdihi
"Wa kulla shayʾin aḥṣaynāhu fī imāmin mubīn"

The gatherer of the Five Divine Presences in his being:
"And everything We have gathered in an evident leader"

وَرَاحِمِ سَائِلِي اسْتِعْدَادَاتِهَا بِنِدَاءِ جُودِهِ "وَمَا أَرْسَلْنَاكَ إِلَّا رَحْمَةً لِلْعَالَمِين"

wa rāḥimi sāʾilī istiʿdādātihā bi-nidāʾi jūdihi
"Wa mā arsalnāka illā raḥmatan li-l-ʿālamīn"
He who shows mercy towards dispositions, in generosity: "We have not sent you but as a mercy to the worlds"

نُقْطَةِ البَسْمَلَةِ الجَامِعَةِ لِمَا يَكُونُ وَلِمَا كَانْ

nuqṭati-l-basmalati-l-jāmiʿati li-mā yakūnu wa li-mā kān
The dot of Opening, encompassing what was and will be

وَنُقْطَةِ الأَمْرِ الجَوَّالَةِ بِدَوَائِرِ الأَكْوَانْ

wa nuqṭati-l-amri-l-jawwālati bi-dawāʾiri-l-akwān
The dot of command, encircling the cosmic cycles

سِرِّ الهُوِيَّةِ الَّتِي فِي كُلِّ شَيْءٍ سَارِيَةٌ

sirri-l-huwiyyati-l-latī fī kulli shayʾin sāriyatun
The secret of the Divine Essence, permeating all things

وَعَنْ كُلِّ شَيْءٍ مُجَرَّدَةٌ وَعَارِيَةٌ

wa ʿan kulli shayʾin mujarradatun wa ʿāriyatun
Yet, from all things abstracted and independent

أَمِينِ اللهِ عَلَى خَزَائِنِ الفَوَاضِلِ وَمُسْتَوْدَعِهَا

amīni Allāhi ʿalā khazāʾini-l-fawāḍili wa mustawdaʿihā
Allah's trustee upon His treasuries, and their vessel

وَمُقَسِّمُهَا عَلَى حَسَبِ القَوَابِلِ وَمُوَزِّعُهَا

wa muqassimuhā ʿalā ḥasabi-l-qawābili wa muwazziʿuhā

And their dispenser according to different molds

كَلِمَةِ الإِسْمِ الأَعْظَمْ وَفَاتِحَةِ الكَنْزِ المُطَلْسَمْ

kalimati-l-ismi-l-Aʿẓam wa fātiḥati-l-kanzi-l-muṭalsam

The word of the Greatest Name and opening of the concealed treasure

المَظْهَرْ الأَتَمِّ الجَامِعِ بَيْنَ العُبُودِيَّةِ وَالرُّبُوبِيَّةِ

al-maẓhar al-atammi-l-jāmiʿi bayna-l-ʿubūdiyyah wa-r-rubūbiyyah

The complete appearance
combining servanthood and lordship

وَالنَّشْأَةِ الأَعَمِّ الشَّامِلِ لِلإِمْكَانِيَّةِ وَالوُجُوبِيَّةِ

wa-n-nashʾati-l-aʿammi-sh-shāmili li-l-imkāniyyah wa-l-wujūbiyyah

The universal form encompassing possibility and necessity

الطَّوْدِ الأَشَمِّ الَّذِي لَمْ يُزَحْزِحْهُ تَجَلِّي التَعَيُّنَاتِ عَنْ مَقَامِ التَمَكُّنِ وَالتَمْكِينْ

a-ṭ-ṭawdi-l-ashammi al-ladhī lam yuzaḥziḥhu tajallī al-taʿayyunāt ʿan maqāmi-t-tamakkuni wa-t-tamkīn

The lofty mountain unshaken, by the manifesting entities, from the firm station

وَالْبَحْرِ الْخِضَمِّ الَّذِي لَمْ تُعَكِّرْهُ جِيَفِ الْغَفَلَاتِ عَنْ صَفَاءِ الْيَقِينِ

wa-l-baḥri-l-khiḍam al-ladhī lam tuʿakkirhu jiyafi-l-ghafalāti ʿan ṣafāʾi-l-yaqīn

The overflowing sea, undistracted from the purity of certainty by the filth of heedlessness

الْقَلَمِ النُّورَانِيِّ الْجَارِي بِمِدَادِ الْحُرُوفِ الْعَالِيَاتْ

al-qalami-n-nūrāniyyi-l-jārī bi-midādi-l-ḥurūfi-l-ʿāliyāt

The luminous pen moving through the ink of lofty letters

وَالنَّفَسِ الرَّحْمَانِي السَّارِي بِمَوَادِ الْكَلِمَاتِ التَّامَّاتْ

wa-n-nafasi-r-raḥmānī as-sārī bi-mawādi-l-kalimāti-t-tāmmāt

The merciful breath permeating the completed words

الْفَيْضِ الْأَقْدَسِ الذَّاتِي الَّذِي تَعَيَّنَتْ بِهِ الْأَعْيَانُ وَاسْتِعْدَادَاتُهَا

al-fayḍi-l-aqdasi-dh-dhātī al-ladhī taʿayyanat bihi-l-aʿyānu wa-stiʿdādātuhā

The holiest manifestation of the Divine Essence, through which entities and their dispositions were designated

وَالْفَيْضِ الْمُقَدَّسِ الصِّفَاتِي الَّذِي تَكَوَّنَتْ بِهِ الْأَكْوَانُ وَاسْتِمْدَادَاتُهَا

wa-l-fayḍi-l-muqaddasi-ṣ-ṣifātī al-ladhī takawwanat bihi-l-akwānu wa-stimdādātuhā

The holy manifestation of the Divine Attributes, through which the universes and their sustenance were formed

مَطْلَعِ شُمُوسِ الذَّاتْ فِي سَمَاءِ الأَسْمَاءِ وَالصِّفَاتْ

maṭlaʿi shumūsi-dh-dhāt fī samāʾi-l-asmāʾi wa-ṣ-ṣifāt

The emergence of the suns of the Divine Essence in the heaven of Divine Names and Attributes

وَمَنْبَعِ نُّورِ الإِفَاضَاتِ فِي رِيَاضِ النِّسَبِ وَالإِضَافَاتْ

wa manbaʿi nūri-l-ifāḍāt fī riyāḍi-n-nisabi wa-l-iḍāfāt

The spring of the light of emanations in the gardens of relationships and associations

خَطِّ الوَحْدَةِ بَيْنَ قَوْسَيّ الأَحَدِيَّةِ وَالوَاحِدِيَّة

khaṭṭi-l-waḥdati bayna qawsiyyi-l-aḥadiyati wa-l-wāḥidiyyah

The line of unity between the two arcs of Divine Singularity and Oneness

وَوَاسِطَةِ التَنَزُّلِ مِنْ سَمَاءِ الأَزَلِيَّةِ إِلَى أَرْضِ الأَبَدِيَّة

wa wāsiṭati-t-tanazzuli min samāʾi-l-azaliyyah ilā arḍi-l-abadiyyah

And the means of descent, from the heaven of pre-eternity to the earth of eternity

النُّسْخَةِ الصُّغْرَى الَّتِي تَفَرَّعَتْ عَنْهَا الكُبْرَى

An-nuskhati-ṣ-ṣughrā al-latī tafarra'at 'anha-l-kubrā
The small version, from which branched the larger

وَالدُّرَّةِ البَيْضَاءِ الَّتِي تَنَزَّلَتْ إِلَى اليَاقُوتَةِ الحَمْرَاءِ

wa-d-durrati-l-bayḍā' al-latī tanazzalat ilā-l-yāqūtati-l-ḥamrā'
And the white pearl that descended to the red ruby

جَوْهَرِ الحَوَادِثِ الإِمْكَانِيَّةِ الَّتِي لَا تَخْلُو عَنِ الحَرَكَةِ وَالسُّكُونْ

jawhari-l-ḥawādithi-l-imkāniyyati-l-latī lā takhlū 'an-il-ḥarakati wa-s-sukūn
The center of possible incidents, indivisible in movement and stillness

وَمَادَّةِ الكَلِمَةِ الفَهْوَانِيَّةِ الطَّالِعَةِ مِنْ كُنْهِ كُنْ إِلَى شَهَادَةِ فَيَكُونْ

wa māddati-l-kalimati-l-fahwāniyyati-ṭ-ṭāli'ati min kunhi Kun ilā shahādati fa-yakūn
And the matter of the uttered Divine Word, rising from the essence of 'Be' to the witnessed testimony of 'It Becomes'

هَيُولَى الصُّوَرِ الَّتِي لَا تَتَجَلَّى بِإِحْدَاهَا مَرَّةً لِإِثْنَيْن

hayūlā aṣ-ṣuwari-l-latī lā tatajallā bi-iḥdāhā marratan li-ithnayn
The mold of forms that does not manifest once to two persons

وَلَا بِصُورَةٍ مِنْهَا لِأَحَدٍ مَرَّتَيْن

wa lā bi-ṣūratin minhā li-aḥadin marratayn

Nor in a single image twice to one person

قُرْآنِ الجَمْعِ الشَّامِلِ لِلْمُمْتَنِعِ وَالعَدِيم

qurʾāni-l-jamʿi-sh-shāmili li-l-mumtaniʿi wa-l-ʿadīm

The *qurʾān* [gathering] of togetherness, encompassing the impossible and deprived

وَفُرْقَانِ الفَرْقِ الفَاصِلِ بَيْنَ الحَادِثِ وَالقَدِيم

wa furqāni-l-farqi-l-fāṣili bayna-l-ḥādithi wa-l-qadīm

And the *furqān* [dispersion] of definite separation between the incidental and eternal

صَائِمِ نَهَارِ "إِنِّي أَبِيتُ عِنْدَ رَبِّي"

ṣāʾimi nahāri "Innī abītu ʿinda rabbī"

He who fasts the morning of "I rest nightly with my Lord"

وَقَائِمِ لَيْلِ "تَنَامُ عَيْنَايَ وَلَا يَنَامُ قَلْبِي"

wa qāʾimi layli "Tanāmu ʿaynāya wa lā yanāmu qalbī"

And who prays the night of "My eyes sleep, but not my heart"

وَاسِطَةِ مَا بَيْنَ الوُجُودِ وَالعَدَمْ: "مَرَجَ البَحْرَيْنِ يَلْتَقِيَانْ"

wāṣiṭati mā bayna-l-wujūdi wa-l-ʿadam: "Maraja-l-bahrayni yaltaqiyān"

The medium between existence and non-existence: "He gathered the two seas whence they meet"

وَرَابِطَةِ تَعَلُّقِ الحُدُوثِ بِالقِدَمْ: "بَيْنَهُمَا بَرْزَخٌ لَا يَبْغِيَان"

wa rābiṭati taʿalluqi-l-ḥudūthi bi-l-qidam: "Baynahumā barzakhun lā yabghiyān"

And the connecting attachment between coming-to-be and eternity: "Between them is a barrier, they do not transgress"

فَذَلِكَ دَفْتَرِ الأَوَّلِ وَالآخِرْ

fa-dhālika daftari-l-awwali-wa-l-ākhir

That [he] is the tome of the First and Last

وَمَرْكَزِ إِحَاطَةِ البَاطِنِ وَالظَّاهِرْ

wa markazi iḥāṭati-l-bāṭini wa-ẓ-ẓāhir

And center of encompassing the Inward and Outward

حَبِيبِكَ الَّذِي اسْتَجْلَيْتَ بِهِ جَمَالَ ذَاتِكَ عَلَى مِنَصَّةِ تَجَلِّيَاتِكْ

ḥabībika al-ladhī istajlayta bihi jamāla Dhātika ʿalā minaṣṣati tajalliyātik

Your beloved through whom You Manifested the Beauty of Your Essence upon the niche of Your Theophanies

وَنَصَبْتَهُ قِبْلَةً لِتَوَجُّهَاتِكَ فِي جَامِعِ جَمِيعِ تَجَلِّيَاتِكَ

wa naṣabtahu qiblatan li-tawajjuhātika fī jāmiʿi jamīʿi tajalliyātik

And whom you established as a direction for Your Gaze in the gathering of all Your Manifestations

وَخَلَعْتَ عَلَيْهِ خِلْعَةَ الصِّفَاتِ وَالأَسْمَاءِ

wa khalaʿta ʿalayhi khilʿata-ṣ-Ṣifāti wa-l-Asmāʾ

Clothing him in the dress of Divine Attributes and Names

وَتَوَّجْتَهُ بِتَاجِ الخِلَافَةِ العُظْمَى

wa tawwajtahu bi-tāji-l-khilāfati-l-ʿuẓmā

And adorning him with the crown of the Greatest Deputyship

وَأَسْرَيْتَ بِجَسَدِهِ يَقَظَةً مِنَ المَسْجِدِ الحَرَامِ إِلَى المَسْجِدِ الأَقْصَى

wa asrayta bi-jasadihi yaqaẓatan mina-l-masjidi-l-ḥarāmi ilā-l-masjidi-l-aqṣā

Taking him on a waking bodily journey from the Sanctified Mosque [Mecca] to the Furthest Mosque [Jerusalem]

حَتَّى انْتَهَى إِلَى سِدْرَةِ المُنْتَهَى وَتَرَقَّى إِلَى قَابِ قَوْسَيْنِ أَوْ أَدْنَى

ḥattā intahā ilā sidrati-l-muntahā wa taraqqā ilā qābi qawsayni aw adnā

Till he reached the Lote Tree, and ascended to Two Bows Length or Less

فَانْسَرَّ وَأَسَرَّ فُؤَادُهُ بِشُهُودِكَ حَيْثُ لَا صَبَاحَ وَلَا مَسَاء

fan-sarra wa asarra fuʾāduhu bi-shuhūdika ḥaythu lā ṣabāḥa wa lā masāʾ

Whence he became joyous, and his heart witnessed You, where there is neither morning nor night

"مَا كَذَبَ الْفُؤَادُ مَا رَأَى"

"Mā kathaba-l-fuʾādu mā raʾā"

"Indeed, the heart does not lie in what it perceives"

وَأَقَرَّ بَصَرُهُ بِوُجُودِكَ حَيْثُ لَا خَلَاءَ وَلَا مَلَاء

wa aqarra baṣaruhu bi-wujūdika ḥaythu lā khalāʾa wa lā malāʾ

His gaze affirming Your Being, where there is neither emptiness nor fullness

"مَا زَاغَ الْبَصَرُ وَمَا طَغَى"

"Mā zāgha-l-baṣaru wa mā ṭaghā"

"Indeed, the sight neither swerves nor transgresses"

صَلِّ اللهُمَّ عَلَيْهِ صَلَاةً يَصِلُ بِهَا فَرْعِي إِلَى أَصْلِي وَبَعْضِي إِلَى كُلِّي

ṣalli Allāhumma ʿalayhi ṣalātan yaṣilu bihā farʿī ilā aṣlī wa baʿḍī ilā kullī

Send prayers upon him, oh Allah, such that my branches reach my root, and my parts to my entirety

لِتَتَّحِدَ ذَاتِي بِذَاتِهِ وَصِفَاتِي بِصِفَاتِه

li-tattaḥida dhātī bi-dhātihi wa ṣifātī bi-ṣifātih
Such that my essence and attributes may unite with his

وَتَقَرَّ الْعَيْنُ بِالعَيْن وَيَفِرَّ الْبَيْنُ مِنَ الْبَيْن

wa taqarra-l-ʿaynu bi-l-ʿayn wa yafirra-l-baynu mina-l-bayn
Whence the eye (I) may find sweetness with the eye (I), and distance flees from the in-between

وَسَلِّمْ عَلَيْهِ سَلَامًا أَسْلَمُ بِهِ فِي مُتَابَعَتِهِ مِنَ التَّخَلُّفْ

wa sallim ʿalayhi salāman aslamu bihi fī mutābaʿatihi mina-l-takhalluf
And send salutations upon him through which I may find safety, in following him, from tarrying

وَأَسْلَمُ فِي طَرِيقِ شَرِيعَتِهِ مِنَ التَّعَسُّفْ

wa aslamu fī ṭarīqi sharīʿatihi mina-t-taʿassuf
Finding safety, in the way of his law, from tyranny

لَأَفْتَحَ بَابَ مَحَبَّتِكَ إِيَّايَ بِمِفْتَاحِ مُتَابَعَتِه

li-aftaḥa bāba maḥabbatika iyyāya bi-miftāḥi mutābaʿatih

Opening the door of Your Love for me through the key of following him

وَأَشْهَدُكَ فِي حَوَاسِّي وَأَعْضَائِي مِنْ مِشْكَاةِ شَرْعِهِ وَطَاعَتِه

wa ash'haduka fī ḥawāssī wa aʿḍāʾī min mishkāti sharʿihi wa ṭāʿatih

Witnessing You in my senses and organs, through the niche of his way and obedience

وَأَدْخُلَ وَرَائَهُ إِلَى حِصْنِ "لَا إِلَه إِلَّا الله"

wa adkhula warāʾahu ilā ḥiṣni "Lā ilāha illā-Allāh"

Entering behind him into the fortress of "There is no god but Allah"

وَفِي أَثَرِهِ إِلَى خَلوَةِ "لِي وَقْتٌ مَعَ الله

wa fī atharihi ilā khalwati "Lī waqtun maʿa-Allāh"

Following his traces into the seclusion of "I have a time, only with my Lord"

إِذْ هُوَ بَابُكَ الَّذِي مَنْ لَمْ يَقْصُدْكَ مِنْهُ سُدَّتْ عَلَيْهِ الطُّرُقَ وَالأَبْوَابْ

idh huwa bābuka al-ladhī man lam yaqṣudka minhu suddat ʿalayhi-ṭ-ṭuruq wa-l-abwāb

For he is Your Gate, through other than whom whoever intends You all their paths and doors are closed

وَرُدَّ بِعَصَا الأَدَبِ إِلَى اسْطَبْلِ الدَّوَابْ

wa rudda bi-ʿaṣa-l-adabi ilā iṣṭabli-d-dawāb
And they will be sent, with the staff of discipline, to the stable of animals

اللهُمَّ يَا رَبِّ يَا مَنْ لَيْسَ حِجَابُهُ إِلَّا النُّور

Allāhumma yā Rabbi yā ma-l-laysa ḥijābuhu illa-n-nūr
Oh Allah, my Lord, whose Veil is naught but Light

وَلَا خَفَائُهُ إِلَّا شِدَّةِ الظُّهُورْ

wa lā khafāʾuhu illā shiddati-ẓ-ẓuhūr
And His Hiddenness is naught but utter manifestation

أَسأَلُكَ بِكَ فِي مَرْتَبَةِ إِطْلَاقِكَ عَنْ كُلِّ تَقْيِيد

asʾaluka bika fī martabati iṭlāqika ʿan kulli taqyīd
I ask You, through You, in the station of Your Absolution from every limitation

الَّتِي تَفْعَلُ فِيهَا مَا تَشَاءُ وَتُرِيد

al-latī tafʿalu fīhā mā tashāʾu wa turīd
At which You do whatever You Will and Decree

وَبِكَشْفِكَ عَنْ ذَاتِكَ بِالعِلْمِ النُّورِيِّ

wa bi-kashfika ʿan dhātika bi-l-ʿilmi-n-nūriyy
Unveiling Your Essence through the luminous knowledge

وَتَحَوُّلِكَ فِي صُوَرِ أَسْمَائِكَ وَصِفَاتِكَ بِالوُجُودِ الصُّورِيِّ

wa taḥawwulika fī ṣuwarī Asmā'ika wa Ṣifātika bi-l-wujūdi-ṣ-ṣūriyy

Turning in the Forms of Your Names and Attributes through the images of existence

أَنْ تُصَلِّيَ عَلَى سَيِّدِنَا مُحَمَّدٍ صَلَاةً

an tuṣalliya ʿalā sayyidinā Muḥammadin ṣalātan

That You send prayers upon our master Muhammad ﷺ

تَكْحَلُ بِهَا أَبْصَارَنَا وَبَصَائِرَنَا بِالنُّورِ المَرْشُوشِ فِي الأَزَلِ

takḥalu bihā abṣāranā wa baṣā'iranā bi-n-nūri-l-marshūshi fi-l-azal

Through which You adorn our sights and insights with the [his] light dispersed in pre-eternity

حَتَّى نَشْهَدَ فَنَاءَ مَا لَمْ يَكُنْ وَبَقَاءَ مَا لَمْ يَزَلْ

ḥattā nashhada fanā'a mā lam yakun wa baqā'a mā lam yazal

So that we may witness the passing of what never was and subsistence of what always has been

وَنَرَى الأَشْيَاءَ كَمَا هِيَ فِي أَصْلِهَا مَعْدُومَةً مَفْقُودَةً

wa nara-l-ashyā'a kamā hiya fī aṣlihā maʿdūmatan mafqūdah

Seeing things as they are in origin: non-existent and lost

وَكَوْنَهَا لَمْ تَشُمَّ رَائِحَةَ الوُجُودِ فَضْلًا عَنْ كَونِهَا مَوْجُودَةْ

wa kawnahā lam tashummā rāʾiḥata-l-wujūdi faḍlan ʿan kawnihā mawjūdah

Never smelling the fragrance of being, much less existing

وَأَخْرِجْنَا اللهُمَّ بِالصَّلَاةِ عَلَيْهِ مِنْ ظُلْمَةِ أَنَانِيَّتِنَا إِلَى النُّورْ

wa akhrijnā Allāhumma bi-ṣ-ṣalāti ʿalayhi min ẓulmati anāniyyatinā ila-n-nūr

And take us, oh Allah, by sending benedictions upon him, from the darkness of our beings to the light

وَمِنْ قَبْرِ جِثْمَانِيَّتِنَا وَجِسْمَانِيَّتِنَا إِلَى جَمْعِ الحَشْرِ وَفَرْقِ النُّشُورْ

wa min qabri jithmāniyyatinā wa jismāniyyatinā ilā jamʿi-l-ḥashri wa farqi-n-nushūr

And from the tomb of our bodies to the gathering of resurrection and dispersion of spreading forth

وَأَفِضْ عَلَيْنَا مِنْ سَمَاءِ تَوْحِيدِكَ إِيَّاكَ مَا تُطَهِّرُنَا بِهِ مِنْ رِجْسِ الشِّرْكِ والإِشْرَاكْ

wa afiḍ ʿalaynā min samāʾi tawḥīdika iyyāka mā tuṭahhirunā bihi min rijsi-sh-shirki wa-l-ishrāk

And unfold upon us, from the Heaven of Your Own Unification, that which purifies us of the filth of polytheism and making partners with you

وأَنْعِشْنا بِالمَوْتَةِ الأُولَى وَالوِلادَةِ الثَّانِيَةْ

wa anʿishnā bi-l-mawtati-l-ūlā wa-l-wilādati-th-thāniyah
Reviving us with the first death and second birth

وَأَحْيِنا بِالحَياةِ البَاقِيَةِ فِي هَذِه الدُّنيا الفَانِيَةْ

wa aḥyinā bi-l-ḥayāti-l-bāqiyati fī hādhihi-d-dunyā-l-fāniyah
Enlivening us with the immortal life in this temporal world

واجْعَل لَنا نُورًا نَمْشِي بِهِ فِي النَّاسْ

wa-jʿal lanā nūran namshī bihi fi-n-nās
And grant us a light through which we may walk among the people

وَنَرَى بِهِ وَجْهَكَ أَيْنَمَا تَوَلَّيْنَا بِدُونِ اشْتِبَاهٍ وَلَا التِبَاسْ

wa narā bihi wajhaka aynamā tawallaynā bi-dūni-shtibāhin wa-la-l-tibās
Gazing, through it [the light], upon Your Face wherever we turn, with neither confusion nor doubt

نَاظِرِينَ بِعَيْنَيِ الجَمْعِ وَالفَرْقْ

nāẓirīna bi-ʿaynayi-l-jamʿi wa-l-farq

Perceiving with the two eyes of gathering and separation

وَفَاصِلِينَ بِحُكْمِ الحَقِّ بَيْنَ البَاطِلِ وَالحَقْ

wa fāṣilīna bi-ḥukmi-l-ḥaqqi bayna-l-bāṭili wa-l-ḥaqq
Separating, with the judgment of the Real, between falsehood and truth

دَالِّينَ بِكَ عَلَيْكْ وَهَادِينَ بِإِذْنِكَ إِلَيْكْ

dāllīna bika ʿalayk wa hādīna bi-idhnika ilayk
Pointing, through You, to You and guiding, with Your Permission, towards You

يَا أَرْحَمَ الرَّاحِمِينْ (ثلاث مرات)

yā arḥama-r-rāḥimīn x 3
Oh, Most Merciful of the merciful x 3

صَلِّ وَسَلِّمْ عَلَى سَيِّدِنَا مُحَمَّدٍ صَلَاةً تَتَقَبَّلُ بِهَا دُعَائَنَا

ṣalli wa sallim ʿalā sayyidinā Muḥammadin ṣalātan tataqabbalu bihā duʿāʾanā
Send Prayers and Salutations upon our master Muhammad, through which You accept our supplication

وَتُحَقِّقُ بِهَا رَجَائَنَا

wa tuḥaqqiqu bihā rajāʾanā
And fulfill our hopes

وَعَلَى آلِهِ آلِ الشُّهودِ وَالعِرْفَانْ

wa ʿalā ālihi āli-sh-shuhūdi wa-l-ʿirfān

And upon his family, the people of witnessing and gnosis

وَأَصْحَابِهِ أَصْحَابِ الذَوْقِ وَالوِجْدَانْ

wa aṣḥābihi aṣḥābi-dhawqi wa-l-wijdān

And his companions, those of taste and ecstasy

مَا انْتَشَرَتْ طُرَّةُ لَيْلِ الكَيَانْ وَأَسْفَرَتْ غُرَّةُ جَبِينِ العِيَانْ

ma-ntasharat ṭurratu layli-l-kayān wa asfarat ghurratu jabīni-l-ʿiyān

As the countenance of being's night spreads, and illumines the eyes of perception

آمين آمين آمين وَالحَمْدُ لله رَبِّ العَالَمِين

āmīn āmīn āmīn wa-l-ḥamdu lillāhi rabbi-l-ʿālamīn

Amen Amen Amen and All Praise is due to Allah the Lord of the Worlds.

بِسْمِ اللّٰهِ الرَّحْمٰنِ الرَّحِيمِ

Bismillāh ar-Raḥmān ar-Raḥīm

In the Name of Allah, Most-Beneficent, Most Merciful

الحَمْدُ لله رَبِّ العَالَمِينَ

وَالصَّلاةُ وَالسَّلامُ عَلَى سَيِّدِنَا مُحَمَّدٍ وَعَلى آلِهِ وَصَحْبِهِ أَجْمَعِينْ

Al-ḥamdu lillāhi Rabbil ʿĀlamīn wa-ṣ-ṣalātu wa-s-salāmu ʿalā sayyidinā Muḥammadin wa ʿalā ālihi wa ṣahbihi ajmaʿīn

All Praise is due to Allah, the Lord of the Worlds. Immense Prayers and Salutations upon our Master Muhammad ﷺ, his family and companions in their entirety.

حِزْبِ الوِقَايَة لِمَنْ أَرَادَ الوِلَايَة

Ḥizbi-l-Wiqāyah li-man arāda-l-Wilāyah

The Litany of Protection for the One Desiring Sainthood[2]

اللهُمَّ يَا حَيُّ يَا قَيُّومُ بِكَ تَحَصَّنْتُ فَاحْمِنِي بِحِمَايَةِ كِفَايَةِ وِقَايَةِ حَقِيقَةِ بُرْهَانِ حِرْزِ أَمَانِ ﴿بِسْمِ اللهِ﴾[3]

Allāhumma yā Ḥayyu yā Qayyūmu bika taḥaṣṣantu fa-ḥminī bi-ḥimāyati kifāyati wiqāyati ḥaqīqati burhāni ḥirzi amāni "Bismillāh"

Oh Allah, the Eternally Living and Self-Standing,

---

[2] This litany is also known as حزب الدور الأعلى (the Litany of Highest Orbit)

[3] الفاتحة 1

through You I seek protection, so protect me with the protection, sufficiency, guardianship, reality, proof, fortress, and safety of "In the Name of Allah."

وَادْخِلْنِي يَا أَوَّلُ يَا آخِرُ فِي مَكْنُونِ غَيْبِ سِرِّ دَائِرَةِ كَنْزِ

﴿مَا شَاءَ اللهُ لَا قُوَّةَ إِلَّا بِاللهِ﴾[4]

wa adkhilnī yā Awwalu yā Ākhiru fī maknūni ghaybi sirri dāʾirati kanzi mā shāʾAllāhu lā quwwata illā bi-llāh

Admit me, oh First and Last, in the essence, unseen, secret, circle, and treasure of 'Whatever Allah Wills, [for indeed], there is no power save through Allah'.

وَاسْبِلْ اللهُمَّ يَا حَلِيمُ يَا سَتَّارُ كَنَفَ سِتْرِ حِجَابِ صِيَانَةِ نَجَاةِ

﴿وَاعْتَصِمُوا بِحَبْلِ اللهِ﴾[5]

wa-sbil Allāhumma yā Ḥalīmu yā Sattāru kanafa sitri ḥijābi ṣiyānati najāti "Wa ʿtaṣimū bi-ḥabli Allāh"

Cast down oh Allah, oh Most-Clement and Concealer of faults the shade, concealment, preservation, and salvation of "Hold onto the Rope of Allah."

وَابْنِ يَا مُحِيطُ يَا قَادِرُ عَلَيَّ سُورَ أَمَانِ إِحَاطَةِ مَجْدِ سُرَادِقِ عِزِّ عَظَمَةِ

ذَلِكَ ﴿خَيْرٌ ذَلِكَ مِنْ آيَاتِ اللهِ﴾[6]

---

4 الكهف 39

5 آل عمران 103

6 الأعراف 26

wa-bni yā Muḥīṭu yā Qādiru ʿalayya sūra amāni iḥāṭati majdi surādiqi ʿizzi ʿaẓamati dhālika khayru dhālika min āyāti Allāh

Build, oh Enveloper and All-Powerful, within me the fence, safety, envelopment, glory, treasuries, exaltedness, and greatness of all that. Indeed, the goodness of that is from among the signs of Allah.

وَأَعِذْنِي يَا رَقِيبُ يَا مُجِيبُ وَاحْرُسْنِي فِي نَفْسِي وَدِينِي وَأَهْلِي وَمَالِي

وَوَلَدِي بِكَلاءَةِ إِعَاذَةِ إِغَاثَةِ ﴿وَلَيْسَ بِضَارِّهِمْ شَيْئًا إِلَّا بِإِذْنِ اللهِ﴾[7]

wa aʿidhnī yā Raqību yā Mujību wa-ḥrusnī fī nafsī wa dīnī wa ahlī wa mālī wa waladī bi-kalāʾati iʿādhati ighāthati "Wa laysa bi-ḍāārrihim shayʾan illā bi-idhni Allāh"

Grant me refuge, Oh All-Watchful and Responder, and guard me in my soul, religion, family, wealth and children through the pasture, refuge, and salvation of "He [satan] will not harm them [believers] save with the permission of Allah."

وَقِنِي يَا مَانِعُ يَا دَافِعُ بِأَسْمَائِكَ وَآيَاتِكَ وَكَلِمَاتِكَ مِنْ شَرِّ الشَّيْطَانِ

وَالسُّلْطَانِ فَإِنْ ظَالِمٌ أَوْ جَبَّارٌ بَغَى عَلَيَّ أَخَذَتْهُ

﴿غَاشِيَةٌ مِنْ عَذَابِ اللهِ﴾[8]

wa qinī yā Māniʿu yā Dāfiʿu bi-asmāʾika wa āyātika wa kalimātika min sharri-sh-shayṭāni wa-s-sulṭāni fa-in

---

7 المجادلة 10

8 يوسف 107

ẓālimun aw jabbārun baghā ʿalayya akhadhathu "Ghāshiyatun min ʿadhābi Allāh"

Protect me, Oh Deterrer and Repeller, through Your Names, Signs and Words, from the evil of Satan and [corrupt] kings. If any of them, transgressor, or oppressor, affronts me, they will be taken by a "calamity from the punishment of Allah."

وَنَجِّنِي يَا مُذِلُّ يَا مُنْتَقِمُ مِنْ عَبِيدِكَ الظَّالِمِينَ فَإِنْ هَمَّ لِي أَحَدٌ مِنْهُم بِسُوءٍ خَذَلَهُ اللهُ ﴿وَخَتَمَ عَلَى سَمْعِهِ وَقَلْبِهِ وَجَعَلَ عَلَى بَصَرِهِ غِشَاوَةً فَمَنْ يَهْدِيهِ مِنْ بَعْدِ اللهِ﴾[9]

wa najjinī yā Mudhillu yā Muntaqimu min ʿabīdika aẓ-ẓālimīna fa-in hamma lī aḥadun minhum bi-sūʾin khadhalahu Allāhu "Wa khatama ʿalā samʿihi wa qalbihi wa jaʿala ʿalā baṣarihi ghishāwatan fa-man yahdīhi min baʿdi Allāh"

Save me, Oh Abaser and Avenger, from your oppressive servants. If any of them seeks to oppress me, Allah will abase them and seal their hearing, heart, and place a veil upon their vision, then who can guide them after Allah?

وَاكْفِنِي يَا قَابِضُ يَا قَهَّارُ خَدِيعَةَ مَكْرِهِمْ وَارْدُدْهُمْ عَنِّي مَذْمُومِينَ مَدْحُورِينَ بِتَخْسِيفِ تَغْيِيرِ تَدْمِيرِ

---

[9] الجاثية 23

﴿فَمَا كَانَ لَهُ مِنْ فِئَةٍ يَنْصُرُونَهُ مِنْ دُونِ اللهِ﴾[10]

wa-kfinī yā Qābiḍu yā Qahhāru khadīʿata makrihim wa-rdud'hum ʿanniya madhmūmīna madḥūrīna bi-takhsīfi taghyīri tadmīri "Fa-mā kāna lahu min fiʾatin yanṣurūnahu min dūni Allāh"

Suffice me, oh Taker and Subduer, from the connivance of their plans, and cast them away from me, in blame and defeat, through the fall, alteration, and destruction of "He [oppressor] had no group to aid him against Allah."

وَأَذِقْنِي يا سُبُّوحُ يَا قُدُّوسُ لَذَّةَ مُنَاجَاةِ

﴿أَقْبِلْ وَلَا تَخَفْ إِنَّكَ مِنَ الآمِنِينَ﴾[11]

wa adhiqnī yā Subbūḥu yā Quddūsu ladhdhata munājāti "Aqbil wa lā takhaf innaka min-al āminīn"

Let me taste, Oh Glorified and Holy One, the sweetness of the soliloquy of "Come near and do not be afraid.

Indeed, you are from those who are granted safety."

وَأَذِقْهُمْ يَا ضَارُّ يَا مُمِيتُ نَكَالَ وَبَالِ زَوَالِ

﴿فَقُطِعَ دَابِرُ الْقَوْمِ الَّذِينَ ظَلَمُوا وَالْحَمْدُ لِلهِ﴾[12]

wa adhiqhum yā Ḍārru yā Mumītu nakāla wabāli zawāli

---

[10] القصص 81

[11] القصص 31

[12] الأنعام 45

"Fa-quṭiʿa dābira-l-qawmi-l-ladhīna ẓalamū wa-l-ḥamdu lillāh"

Let them taste, Oh Afflicter and Granter of Death, the punishment, sickness, and annihilation of "The traces of the oppressive folk were cut, and all Praise is due to Allah."

وَآمِنِّي يَا سَلَامُ يَا مُؤْمِنُ يَا مُهَيْمِنُ صَوْلَةَ جَوْلَةِ دَوْلَةِ الأَعْدَاءِ بِغَايَةِ بِدَايَةِ ﴿لَهُمُ الْبُشْرَىٰ فِي الْحَيَاةِ الدُّنيَا وَفِي الْآخِرَةِ لَا تَبْدِيلَ لِكَلِمَاتِ اللَّهِ﴾[13]

wa āminnī yā Salāmu yā Muʾminu yā Muhayminu ṣawlata jawlati dawlati-l-aʿdāʾi bi-ghāyati bidāyati "Lahumu-l-bushrā fī-l-ḥayāti-d-dunyā wa fī-l-ākhirati lā tabdīla li-kalimāti Allāh"

Grant me safety, Oh Peace and Overpowering One, from the assault, patrol, and governance of enemies through the destination and beginning of "They have the glad tiding in this lower world and hereafter. Indeed, there is no alteration to the Words of Allah."

وَتَوِّجْنِي يَا عَظِيمُ يَا مُعِزُّ بِتَاجِ مَهَابَةِ كِبْرِيَاءِ جَلَالِ سُلطَانِ مَلَكُوتِ عِزِّ عَظَمَةِ ﴿وَلَا يَحْزُنكَ قَوْلُهُمْ إِنَّ الْعِزَّةَ لِلَّهِ﴾

wa tawwijnī yā ʿAẓīmu yā Muʿizzu bi-tāji mahābati kibriyāʾi jalāli sulṭāni malakūti ʿizzi ʿaẓamati "Wa lā yaḥzunka qawluhum inna-l-ʿizzata lillāh"

---

[13] يونس 64

Crown me, Oh Great One and Exalter, with the crown of splendor, pride, majesty, authority, kingship, exaltedness, and greatness of "Let not their statement sadden you. Indeed, exaltedness belongs to Allah."

وَأَلْبِسْنِي يَا جَلِيلُ يَا كَبِيرُ خِلْعَةَ جَلَالِ جَمَالِ كَمَالِ إِقْبَالِ ﴿فَلَمَّا رَأَيْنَهُ
أَكْبَرْنَهُ وَقَطَّعْنَ أَيْدِيَهُنَّ وَقُلْنَ حَشَ لِلّٰهِ﴾[14]

wa albisnī yā Jalīlu yā Kabīru khilʿata jalāli jamāli kamāli iqbāli "Fa-lammā raʾaynahu akbarnahu wa qaṭṭaʿna aydiyahunna wa qulna ḥāsha lillāh"

Clothe me, Oh Most Sublime and Grandiose with the cloth, majesty, beauty, perfection and welcome of "When they saw him, they hailed him and cut off their hands, proclaiming: 'God forbid'."

وَأَلْقِ يَا عَزِيزُ يَا وَدُودُ عَلَيَّ مَحَبَّةً مِنْكَ فَتَنْقَادُ وَتَخْضَعُ لِي بِهَا قُلُوبَ
عِبَادِكَ بِالْمَحَبَّةِ وَالْمَعَزَّةِ وَالْمَوَدَّةِ مِنْ تَعْطِيفِ تَلْطِيفِ تَأْلِيفِ
﴿يُحِبُّونَهُمْ كَحُبِّ اللّٰهِ وَالَّذِينَ آمَنُوا أَشَدُّ حُبًّا لِلّٰهِ﴾[15]

wa alqi yā ʿAzīzu yā Wadūdu ʿalayya maḥabbatan minka fa-tanqādu wa takhḍaʿu lī bihā qulūba ʿibādika bi-l-maḥabbati wa-l-maʿazzati wa-l-mawwadati min taʿṭīfi talṭīfi taʾlīfi "Yuḥibbūnahum ka-ḥubbi Allāh wa-l-ladhīna āmanū ashaddu ḥubban lillāh"

Cast down, Oh Most Honorable and Most Loving

---

[14] يوسف 31

[15] البقرة 165

One, upon me a love from You, whence the hearts of Your servants will be driven to and submit to me, with love, exaltedness and amor, from the gentleness, softness, and amiability of "They love them like the love of Allah. Indeed, those who believe are more intense in their love for Allah."

وَأَظْهِرِ اللهُمَّ عَلَيَّ يَا ظَاهِرُ يَا بَاطِنُ آثَارَ أَسْرَارِ أَنْوَارِ ﴿يُحِبُّهُمْ وَيُحِبُّونَهُ أَذِلَّةٍ عَلَى الْمُؤْمِنِينَ أَعِزَّةٍ عَلَى الْكَافِرِينَ يُجَٰهِدُونَ فِي سَبِيلِ اللهِ﴾[16]

wa aẓhiri Allāhumma ʿalayya yā Ẓāhiru yā Bāṭinu āthāra asrāri anwāri "Yuḥibbuhum wa yuḥibbūnahu adhillatin ʿalā-l-muʾminīna aʿizzatin ʿalā-l-kāfirīna yujāhidūna fī sabīli Allāh"

Manifest upon me, Oh Allah, Most Manifest and Most Inward, traces of the secrets of the lights of "He loves them, and they love Him, [they are] humble towards the believers, proud against the disbelievers, struggling in the way of Allah."

وَوَجِّهْ اللهُمَّ يَا صَمَدُ يَا نُورُ وَجْهِيَ بِصَفَاءِ جَمَالِ أُنْسِ إِشْرَاقِ ﴿فَإِنْ حَآجُّوكَ فَقُلْ أَسْلَمْتُ وَجْهِيَ لِلهِ﴾[17]

wa wajjih Allāhumma yā Ṣamadu yā Nūru wajhiya bi-ṣafāʾi jamāli unsi ishrāqi "Fa-in ḥāājjūka fa-qul aslamtu wajhiya lillāh"

Direct my face, oh Allah the Self-Sufficient and Light,

---

16 المائدة 54

17 آل عمران 20

through the purity, beauty, intimacy, and illumination of "If they debate with you, say 'I have submitted my face to Allah'."

وَجَمِّلْنِي يَا بَدِيعَ السَّمَاوَاتِ وَالأَرْضِ يَا ذَا الجَلالِ وَالإِكْرَامِ بِالفَصَاحَةِ وَالبَلَاغَةِ وَالبَرَاعَةِ ﴿وَاحْلُلْ عُقْدَةً مِنْ لِسَانِي يَفْقَهُوا قَوْلِي﴾[18] بِرِقَّةِ رَأْفَةِ رَحْمَةِ ﴿ثُمَّ تَلِينُ جُلُودُهُمْ وَقُلُوبُهُمْ إِلَى ذِكْرِ اللهِ﴾[19]

wa jammilnī yā Badīʿa-s-samāwāti wa-l-arḍi yā Dha-l-Jalāli wa-l-Ikrām bi-l-faṣāḥati wa-l-balāghati wa-l-barāʿati "Wa-ḥlul ʿuqdatan mi-l-lisānī yafqahū qawlī" bi-riqqati raʾfati raḥmati "Thumma talīnu julūduhum wa qulūbuhum ilā dhikri Allāh"

Beautify me, Oh Innovator of the heavens and earth, One of Exaltedness and Generosity, with the clarity, eloquence, and excellence of "And untie a knot from my tongue that they may understand my speech" with the gentleness, kindness, and mercy of "Then their skins and hearts soften in the remembrance of Allah."

وَقَلِّدْنِي يَا شَدِيدَ البَطْشِ يَا جَبَّارُ يَا قَهَّارُ سَيْفَ الهَيْبَةِ وَالقُوَّةِ وَالشِّدَّةِ وَالمَنَعَةِ مِنْ بَأْسِ جَبَرُوتِ عِزَّةِ عَظَمَةِ

---

18 طه 27

19 الزمر 23

﴿وَمَا النَّصْرُ إِلَّا مِنْ عِنْدِ اللهِ﴾[20]

wa qallidniya yā Shadīda-l-Baṭshi yā Jabbāru yā Qahhāru sayfa-l-haybati wa-l-quwwati wa-sh-shiddati wa-l-manaʿati min baʾsi jabarūti ʿizzati ʿaẓamati "Wa ma-n-naṣru illā min ʿindi Allāh"

Dress me, oh Swift in Punishment, Overpowering One and Subduer, with the sword of awe, strength, power, and deterrence, from the clout, exaltedness, and greatness of "Indeed, victory is naught save from Allah."

وَأَدِمْ عَلَيَّ يَا بَاسِطُ يَا فَتَّاحُ بَهْجَةَ مَسَرَّةِ ﴿رَبِّ اشْرَحْ لِي صَدْرِي وَيَسِّرْ لِي أَمْرِي﴾[21] بِعَوَاطِفِ لَطَائِفِ ﴿أَلَمْ نَشْرَحْ لَكَ صَدْرَكَ﴾[22] بِأَشَائِرِ بَشَائِرِ ﴿وَيَوْمَئِذٍ يَفْرَحُ الْمُؤْمِنُونَ بِنَصْرِ اللهِ﴾[23]

wa adim ʿalayya yā Bāṣiṭu yā Fattāḥu bahjata masarrati "Rabbi-shraḥ lī ṣadrī wa yassir lī amrī" bi-ʿawāṭifi laṭāʾifi "A-lam nashraḥ laka ṣadrak" bi-ashāʾiri bashāʾiri "Wa yawmaʾidhin yafraḥu-l-muʾminūna bi-naṣri Allāh"

Keep upon me, Oh Expander and Opener, the happiness and joy of "Oh my Lord, expand my chest and facilitate my affair for me," with the emotions and subtleties of "Did We not expand your chest for you", and allusions and glad tidings of

---

20 الأنفال 10

21 طه 25

22 الشرح 1

23 الروم 4

"On that day, the believers rejoice with the victory of Allah"

وَأَنْزِلِ اللهُمَّ يَا لَطِيفُ يَا رَؤُوفُ بِقَلْبِيَ الإِيمَانَ وَالاطْمِئْنَانَ وَالسَّكِينَةَ وَالوَقَارَ لِأَكُونَ مِنَ

﴿الَّذِينَ آمَنُوا وَتَطْمَئِنُّ قُلُوبُهُمْ بِذِكْرِ اللهِ﴾

wa anzili Allāhumma yā Laṭīfu yā Raʾūfu bi-qalbiya-l-īmāna wa-l-iṭmiʾnāna wa-s-sakīnata wa-l-waqāra li-akūna min "Al-ladhīna āmanū wa taṭmaʾinnu qulūbuhum bi-dhikri Allāh"

Cast down in my heart, Oh Allah Most Gentle and Most Kind, faith, tranquility, stillness, and regality such that I become from "Those who believe, and their hearts find tranquility in the remembrance of Allah."

وَافْرِغْ عَلَيَّ يَا صَبُورُ يَا شَكُورُ صَبْرَ الَّذِينَ تَدَرَّعُوا بِثَبَاتِ يَقِينِ تَمْكِينِ

﴿كَمْ مِنْ فِئَةٍ قَلِيلَةٍ غَلَبَتْ فِئَةً كَثِيرَةً بِإِذْنِ اللهِ﴾[24]

wa afrigh ʿalayya yā Ṣabūru yā Shakūru ṣabra al-ladhīna tadarraʿū bi-thabāti yaqīni tamkīni "Kam min fiʾatin qalīlatin ghalabat fiʾatan kathīratan bi-idhni Allāh"

Empty upon me, Oh Most Patient and Most Grateful, the patience of those who fortified themselves with the firmness, certainty, and ability of "How many a few defeated many with the permission of Allah."

---

[24] البقرة 249

وَاحْفَظْنِيَ يَا حَفِيظُ يَا وَكِيلُ مِنْ بَيْنِ يَدَيَّ وَمِنْ خَلْفِي وَعَنْ يَمِينِي وَعَنْ شِمَالِي وَمِنْ فَوْقِي وَمِنْ تَحْتِي بِوُجودِ شُهودِ جُنودِ ﴿لَهُ مُعَقِّبَاتٌ مِنْ بَيْنِ يَدَيهِ وَمِنْ خَلْفِهِ يَحْفَظُونَهُ مِنْ أَمْرِ اللهِ﴾[25]

wa-ḥfaẓniya yā Ḥafīẓu yā Wakīlu min bayni yadayya wa min khalfi wa ʿan yamīnī wa ʿan shimālī wa min fawqī wa min taḥtī bi-wujūdi shuhūdi junūdi "Lahu muʿaqqibātun min bayni yadayhi wa min khalfihi yaḥfaẓūnahu min amri Allāh"

Guard me, Oh Guardian and Trustee, from between my hands, behind me, on my right and left, from above and below me, with the being, witnessing and soldiers of "He has protectors between his hands and from behind him that protect him, by the command of Allah."

وَثَبِّتْ اللهُمَّ يَا قَائِمُ يَا دَائِمُ قَدَمَيَّ كَمَا ثَبَّتَّ القَائِلَ ﴿وَكَيْفَ أَخَافُ مَا أَشْرَكْتُمْ وَلَا تَخَافُونَ أَنَّكُمْ أَشْرَكْتُمْ بِاللهِ﴾[26]

wa thabbit Allāhumma yā Qāʾimu yā Dāʾimu qadamayya ka-mā thabbatta-l-qāʾila "Wa kayfa akhāfu mā ashraktum wa lā takhāfūna annakum ashraktum billāh"

Make firm, Oh Ever standing and Subsistent, my feet as you have affirmed the one who said: "How can I fear what you posit as partners while you are not afraid that you made partners with Allah."

---

25 الرعد 11

26 الأنعام 81

وَانْصُرْنِي يَا نِعْمَ الْمَوْلَى وَيَا نِعْمَ النَّصِيرُ عَلَى أَعْدَائِي نَصْرَ الَّذِي قِيلَ لَهُ ﴿أَتَتَّخِذُنَا هُزُوًا قَالَ أَعُوذُ بِاللهِ﴾[27]

wa-nṣurnī yā Niʿma-l-Mawlā wa yā Niʿma-n-Naṣīr ʿalā aʿdāʾiya naṣra al-ladhī qīla lahu "Atattakhidhunā huzuwan qāla aʿūdhu billāh"

Grant me victory, Oh Best of Guardians and Givers of victory, upon my enemies; the triumph of one who was told: "Do you mock us? He said: 'I seek refuge in Allah [from that].'"

وَأَيِّدْنِيَ يَا طَالِبُ يَا غَالِبُ بِتَأْيِيدِ نَبِيِّكَ سَيِّدِنَا مُحَمَّدٍ صَلَّى اللهُ عَلَيْهِ وَسَلَّمْ الْمُؤَيَّدِ بِتَعْزِيزِ تَوْقِيرِ ﴿إِنَّا أَرْسَلْنَاكَ شَاهِداً وَمُبَشِّراً وَنَذِيراً﴾ ﴿لِتُؤْمِنُوا بِاللهِ﴾[28]

wa ayyidniya yā Ṭālibu yā Ghālibu bi-taʾyīdi nabiyyika sayyidinā Muḥammadin ṣallā Allāhu ʿalayhi wa sallama-l-muʾayyadi bi-taʿzīzi tawqīri "Innā arsalnāka shāhidan wa mubashshiran wa nadhīran li-tuʾminū billāh"

Aid me, Oh Seeker and Overcomer, with the aid of Your Prophet, our master Muhammad ﷺ, he who is aided with the exaltedness and regality of "Indeed, We have sent you as a witness, giver of glad tidings and a warner. That you may believe in Allah"

---

[27] البقرة 67

[28] الفتح 8–9

وَاكْفِنِي يَا كَافِي يَا شَافِي الأَعدَاءَ وَالأَسْوَاءَ بِعَوَائِدِ فَوَائِدِ ﴿لَوْ أَنْزَلْنَا هَذَا القُرْآنَ عَلَى جَبَلٍ لَرَأَيْتَهُ خَاشِعًا مُتَصَدِّعًا مِنْ خَشْيَةِ اللهِ﴾[29]

wa-kfinī yā Kāfī yā Shāfī al-aʿdāʾa wa-l-aswāʾa bi-ʿawāʾidi fawāʾidi "Law anzalnā hādha-l-Qurʾāna ʿalā jabalin la-raʾaytahu khāshiʿan mutaṣaddiʿan min khashyati Allāh"

Suffice me, Oh Most Sufficient and Most Healing, from enemies and all evil, with the returns and benefits of "Had We brought this Quran down on a mountain you would have seen it solemn and trembling in consciousness of Allah."

وَامْنُنْ عَلَيَّ يَا وَهَّابُ يَا رَزَّاقُ بِحُصُولِ وُصولِ قَبولِ تَيسيرِ تَسْخيرِ ﴿كُلُوا وَاشْرَبُوا مِنْ رِزقِ اللهِ﴾[30]

wa-mnun ʿalayya yā Wahhābu yā Razzāqu bi-ḥuṣūli wuṣūli qabūli taysīri taskhīri "Kulū wa-shrabū mi-r-rizqi Allāh"

Bless me, Oh Giver and Sustainer, with the obtainment, reach, acceptance, facilitation, and dispensation of "Eat and drink from the sustenance of Allah."

وَتَوَلَّنِي يَا وَلِيُّ يَا عَلِيُّ بِالوَلَايَةِ وَالعِنَايَةِ وَالرِّعَايَةِ وَالسَّلَامَةِ بِمَزِيدِ

---

[29] الحشر 21

[30] البقرة 60

إِيرَادِ إِسْعَادِ إِمْدَادِ ﴿ذَٰلِكَ مِنْ فَضْلِ اللهِ﴾[31]

wa tawallanī yā Waliyyu yā ʿAliyyu bi-l-walāyati wa-l-ʿināyati wa-r-riʿāyati wa-s-salāmati bi-mazīdi īrādi isʿādi imdādi "Dhālika min faḍli Allāh"

Entrust me to You, Oh Trustee and Most Lofty with sainthood, attentiveness, care and safety with an increase, happiness, and providence of "That is from the Bounty of Allah."

وَأَكْرِمْنِي يَا غَنِيُّ يَا كَرِيمُ بِالسَّعَادَةِ وَالكَرَامَةِ وَالمَغْفِرَةِ كَمَا أَكْرَمْتَ ﴿الَّذِينَ يَغُضُّونَ أَصْوَاتَهُمْ عِنْدَ رَسُولِ اللهِ﴾[32]

wa akrimnī yā Ghaniyyu yā Karīmu bi-s-saʿādati wa-l-karāmati wa-l-maghfirati ka-mā akramta "Al-ladhīna yaghuḍḍūna aṣwātihim ʿinda rasūlillāh"

Ennoble me, Oh Most Abundant and Most Generous, with happiness, generosity, and forgiveness as you have ennobled "Those who lower their voices in [the presence of] the Messenger of Allah [ﷺ]."

وَتُبْ عَلَيَّ يَا تَوَّابُ يَا رَحِيمُ تَوْبَةً نَصُوحاً لِأَكُونَ مِنَ الَّذِينَ ﴿إِذَا فَعَلُوا فَٰحِشَةً أَوْ ظَلَمُوا أَنْفُسَهُمْ ذَكَرُوا اللهَ فَاسْتَغْفَرُوا لِذُنُوبِهِمْ وَمَنْ يَغْفِرُ الذُّنُوبَ إِلَّا اللهُ﴾[33]

---

31 يوسف 38

32 الحجرات 3

33 آل عمران 135

wa tub ʿalayya yā Tawwābu yā Raḥīmu tawbatan naṣūḥan li-akūna min-al-ladhīna "Idhā faʿalū fāḥishatan aw ẓalamū anfusahum dhakarū Allāha fa-staghfarū li-dhunūbihim wa ma-y-yaghfiru-dh-dhunūba illā Allāh"

Accept my repentance, Oh Most Forgiving and Most Merciful. A repentance true and sincere, so I may be from those "Who if they commit a sin or oppress themselves, they remember Allah and seek forgiveness for their sins. Indeed, who forgives sins but Allah."

وَالزِمْنِي يَا وَاحِدُ يَا أَحَدُ كَلِمَةَ التَّقْوَى كَمَا أَلْزَمْتَ حَبِيبِكَ سَيِّدِنَا مُحَمَّدٍ صَلَّى اللهُ عَلَيهِ وَسَلَّمْ حَيْثُ قُلْتَ ﴿فَاعْلَمْ أَنَّهُ لَا إِلَهَ إِلَّا اللهُ﴾[34]

wa alzimnī yā Wāḥidu yā Aḥadu kalimata-t-taqwā ka-mā alzamta ḥabībika sayyidinā Muḥammadin ṣallā Allāhu ʿalayhi wa sallam ḥaythu qulta "Fa-ʿlam annahu lā ilāha illā Allāh"

Tether me, Oh One and Singular, to the word of piety, as You have commanded Your Beloved our master Muhammad ﷺ when you said: "Know that there is no god but Allah."

وَاخْتِمْ لِي يَا رَحْمَنُ يَا رَحِيمُ بِحُسْنِ خَاتِمَةِ النَّاجِينَ وَالرَّاجِينَ ﴿قُلْ يَا عِبَادِيَ الَّذِينَ أَسْرَفُوا عَلَى أَنْفُسِهِمْ لَا تَقْنَطُوا مِنْ رَحْمَةِ اللهِ﴾[35]

---

34 محمد 19

35 الزمر 53

wa-khtim lī yā Raḥmānu yā Raḥīmu bi-ḥusni khātimati-n-nājīna wa-r-rājīna "Qul yā ʿibādiya al-ladhīna asrafū ʿalā anfusihim lā taqnaṭū mi-r-raḥmati Allāh"

Seal for me, Oh Most Merciful and Most Beneficent, with the beautiful seal of those who are saved and hopeful "Say My Servants who have transgressed against themselves do not despair of the Mercy of Allah."

وَأَسْكِنِّي يَا سَمِيعُ يَا عَلِيمُ يَا قَرِيبُ جَنَّةً أُعِدَّتْ لِلْمُتَّقِينَ دَعْوَاهُمْ فِيهَا ﴿سُبْحَٰنَكَ اللَّهُمَّ وَتَحِيَّتُهُمْ فِيهَا سَلَٰمٌ وَءَاخِرُ دَعْوَاهُمْ أَنِ الْحَمْدُ لِلَّهِ﴾[36]

wa askinniya yā Samīʿu yā ʿAlīmu yā Qarību jannatan uʿiddat li-l-muttaqīna daʿwāhum fīhā "Subḥānaka Allāhumma wa taḥiyyatuhum fīhā salāmun wa ākhiru daʿwāhum ani-l-ḥamdu lillāh"

Place me, Oh All-Hearing, All Knowing and Nearest, in a paradise that has been prepared for the pious, wherein their supplication is "Glory be to You, oh Allah. Their greeting therein is 'peace' and the last of their supplications is 'All praise is due to Allah.'"

يَا اللهُ يَا اللهُ يَا اللهُ يَا اللهُ يَا رَبُّ يَا نَافِعُ يَا رَحْمَنُ يَا رَحِيمُ اسْأَلُكَ بِحُرْمَةِ هَذِهِ الأَسْمَاءِ وَالآيَاتِ وَالكَلِمَاتِ سُلطَاناً نَصِيراً وَرِزْقاً كَثِيراً

---

36 يونس 10

وَقَلْباً قَرِيرَاً وَقَبْرَاً مُنِيرَاً وَحِسَاباً يَسِيرَاً وَأَجْرَاً كَبِيرَاً وَصَلَّى اللهُ عَلَى سَيِّدِنَا مُحَمَّدٍ وَعَلَى آلِهِ وَصَحْبِهِ أَجْمَعِين

yā Allāhu yā Allāhu yā Allāhu yā Allāhu yā Rabbu yā Nāfiʿu yā Raḥmānu yā Raḥīmu asʾaluka bi-ḥurmati hādhihi-l-Asmāʾi wa-l-āyāti wa-l-kalimāt sulṭānan naṣīran wa rizqan kathīran wa qalban qarīran wa qabran munīran wa ḥisāban yasīran wa ajran kabīran wa ṣallā Allāhu ʿalā sayyidinā Muḥammadin wa ʿalā ālihi wa ṣaḥbihi ajmaʿīn

Oh, Allah x 4, My Lord, Giver of Benefit, Most Merciful and Most Beneficent, I ask you by the sanctity of these Names, verses, and words a victory-giving authority, abundant sustenance, soft heart, illuminated grave, easy judgment and bountiful reward. And send Your prayers upon our master Muhammad ﷺ.

بِسْمِ اللَّهِ الرَّحْمَٰنِ الرَّحِيمِ

Bismillāh ar-Raḥmān ar-Raḥīm

In the Name of Allah, Most-Beneficent, Most Merciful

الحَمْدُ لله رَبِّ العَالَمِينَ

وَالصَّلاةُ وَالسَّلامُ عَلَى سَيِّدِنَا مُحَمَّدٍ وَعَلى آلِهِ وَصَحْبِهِ أَجْمَعِينْ

Al-ḥamdu lillāhi Rabbil ʿĀlamīn wa-ṣ-Ṣalātu wa-s-Salāmu ʿalā sayyidinā Muḥammadin wa ʿalā ʾālihi wa ṣaḥbihi ajmaʿīn

All Praise is due to Allah, the Lord of the Worlds. Immense Prayers and Salutations upon our Master Muhammad ﷺ, his family and companions in their entirety.

أَوْرَادُ الأُسْبُوع

Awrādu-l-Usbūʿ

Litanies for Days of the Week[37]

---

[37] Note: Ibn ʿArabi states that the litany for the night should precede the day, according to the lunar calendar, where the day officially begins after *maghrib* prayer. For example, the litany for the night of Sunday should be read on Saturday evening, after *maghrib* prayer until *fajr*. The litany for the day can be read anytime from *fajr* until *maghrib*. The litanies have been organized accordingly here.

لَيْلَةُ الأَحَدْ

Laylatu-l-Aḥad

The Night of Sunday

اللهُمَّ أَنْتَ المُحِيطُ بِغَيْبِ كُلِّ شَاهِدٍ وَالمُسْتَوْلِي عَلَى بَاطِنِ كُلِّ ظَاهِرٍ، إِلَهِي أَسْأَلُكَ بِوَجْهِكَ الكَرِيمِ الَّذِي عَنَتْ لَهُ الوُجُوهْ، وَبِنُورِكَ الَّذِي شَخَصَتْ إِلَيْهِ الأَبْصَارْ، أَنْ تَهْدِيَنِي إِلَى صِرَاطِكَ الخَاصِ هِدَايَةً تَصْرِفُ بِهَا وَجْهِي عَمَّنْ سِوَاكْ

Allāhumma anta-l-Muḥīṭu bi-ghaybi kulli shāhidin wa-l-Mustawlī ʿalā bāṭini kulli ẓāhirin, ilāhi asʾaluka bi-Wajhika-l-Karīm al-ladhī ʿanat lahu-l-wujūh, wa bi-Nūrika al-ladhī shakhaṣat ilayhi-l-abṣār, an tahdiyanī ilā Ṣirāṭika-l-Khāṣ hidāyatan taṣrifu bihā wajhiya ʿamman siwāk

Oh Allah, You are the One who Envelops the unseen of every testimony and the One who overwhelms the inward of every outward. Oh Allah, I ask You by Your Noble Countenance, towards which all faces are overcome, and by Your Light, under which all gazes are directed, that You guide me to Your Special Path, a guidance through which You turn my face away from all other than You

يَا مَنْ هُوَ الهُو المُطْلَقْ وَأَنَا العَبْدُ المُقَيَّدْ، يَا مَنْ لَا إِلَهَ إِلَّا هُو، إِلَهِي شَأْنُكَ قَهْرَ الأَعْدَاءِ وَقَمْعَ الجَبَابِرَة، أَسْأَلُكَ مَدَداً مِنْ عِزَّةِ أَسْمَائِكَ القَهْرِيَّةِ يَمْنَعُنِي مِنْ كُلِّ مَنْ أَرَادَنِي بِسُوءٍ

حَتَّى أَكُفَّ بِهِ يَدَ البَاغِينَ وَاقْطَعُ بِهِ دَابِرَ الظَّالِمِينْ

Yā man Huwa-l-Hū al-Muṭlaq wa ana-l-ʿabdu-l-muqayyad, yā man lā ilāha illā Hū, ilāhī shaʾnuka qahra-l-aʿdāʾ wa qamʿa-l-jabābirah, asʾaluka madadan min ʿizzati Asmāʾika-l-Qahriyyati yamnaʿunī min kulli man arādanī bi-sūʾin ḥattā akuffa bihi yada-l-bāghīna wa aqṭaʿa bihi dābira-ẓ-ẓālimīn

Oh You, who is the Absolute He and I am the bounded servant, oh You beside whom there is no god. Oh Allah, Your Affair is to subdue enemies and crush tyrants. I ask You a providence from the exaltedness of Your Subduing Names to guard me from all those who wish me harm, so that I may deter through it the hands of transgressors and cut off the way of oppressors

وَمَلِّكْنِي نَفْسِي مُلْكاً يُقَدِّسُنِي عَنْ كُلِّ خُلُقٍ سَيِّءٍ وَاهْدِنِي إِلَيْكَ، يَا هَادِي إِلَيْكَ يَرجِعُ كُلَّ شَيْءٍ وَأَنْتَ بِكُلِّ شَيْءٍ مُحِيطْ، ﴿وَهُوَ القَاهِرُ فَوْقَ عِبَادِهِ وَهُوَ الحَكِيمُ الخَبِيرْ﴾[38]

wa mallikni nafsī mulkan yuqaddisunī ʿan kulli khuluqin sayyiʾin wa hdinī ilayk, yā Hādī ilayka yarjiʿu kulla shayʾ wa anta bi-kulli shayʾin Muḥīṭ, wa "Huwa-l-Qāhiru fawqa ʿibādihi wa Huwa-l-Ḥakīmu-l-Khabīr"

Grant me a dominion over my soul that sanctifies me from every lowly trait and guide me to You. Oh, He who guides, to You returns everything and You

---

[38] الأنعام 18

surround all things. "And He is the Subduer over His servants, and He is the All-Wise, All-Aware"

إِلَهي أَنْتَ القَائِمُ عَلَى كُلِّ نَفْسٍ وَالقَيُّومُ عَلَى كُلِّ مَعْنىً وَحِسّ، قَدَرْتَ فَقَهَرْتَ وَعَلِمْتَ فَقَدَّرْتَ فَلَكَ القُدْرَةُ وَالقَهْرُ وَبِيَدِكَ الخَلْقُ وَالأَمْرُ وَأَنْتَ مَعَ كُلِّ شَيءٍ قَرِيبٍ وَبِكُلِّ شَيءٍ مُحِيط

Ilāhī anta-l-Qā'imu 'alā kulli nafsin wa-l-Qayyūmu 'alā kulli ma'nan wa ḥiss, qadarta fa-qaharta wa 'alimta fa-qaddarta fa-laka-l-qudratu wa-l-qahru wa biyadika-l-khalqu wa-l-amru wa anta ma'a kulli shay'in Qarībin wa bi-kulli shay'in Muḥīṭ

Oh Allah, You are the who attends to every soul and establishes every meaning and sense. You overpowered and subdued. You have knowledge and established measures. To You belong power and compulsion, and in Your Hands is creation and command. You are to everything Near and Enveloping.

إِلَهي أَسْأَلُكَ مَدَداً مِنْ أَسْمَائِكَ القَهْرِيَّةِ تُقَوِّي بِهَا قُوَايَ القَلْبِيَّةِ وَالقَالِبِيَّةِ حَتَّى لَا يَلْقَانِي صَاحِبُ قَلْبٍ إِلَّا انْقَلَبَ عَلَى عَقِبَيْهِ مَقْهُورا

Ilāhī as'aluka madadan min Asmā'ika-l-Qahriyyati tuqawwī bihā quwāiya-l-qalbiyyati wa-l-qālibiyyati ḥattā lā yalqānī ṣāḥibu qalbin illa-nqalaba 'alā 'aqibayhi maqhūrā

Oh Allah, I ask You a providence from Your Subduing Names to strengthen my faculties, in heart and form, such that no one with overturned [disposition] meets me except that they turn back subdued [into goodness].

وَأَسْأَلُكَ إِلَهِي لِسَاناً نَاطِقَاً وَقَوْلاً صَادِقَاً وَفَهْماً لَائِقَاً وَسِرَّاً ذَائِقَاً
وَقَلْبَاً قَابِلاً وَعَقْلاً عَاقِلاً وَفِكْراً مُشْرِقَاً وَطَرْفَاً مُطْرِفَاً وَشَوْقَاً مُقْلِقَاً
وَتَوْقَاً مُحْرِقَاً وَوَجْداً مُطْبِقَاً وَهَبْ لِي يَداً قَادِرَةً وَقُوَّةً قَاهِرَةً وَعَيْنَاً
حَامِيَةً وَنَفْساً مُطْمَئِنَّةً وَجَوَارِحَاً لِطَاعَتِكَ غَيْرَ مُتَوَانِيَةٍ وَقَدِّسْنِي
لِلقُدُومِ عَلَيْكَ وَارْزُقْنِي التَقَدُّمِ إِلَيْك

wa as'aluka Ilāhī lisānan nāṭiqan wa qawlan ṣādiqan wa fahman lā'iqan wa sirran dhā'iqan wa qalban qābilan wa 'aqlan 'āqilan wa fikran mushriqan wa ṭarfan muṭrifan wa shawqan muqliqan wa tawqan muḥriqan wa wajdan muṭbiqan wa hab lī yadan qādiratan wa quwwatan qāhiratan wa 'aynan ḥāmiyatan wa nafsan muṭma'innatan wa jawāriḥan li-ṭā'atika ghayra mutawāniyatin wa qaddisnī li-l-qudūmi 'alayka wa-rzuqnī-t-taqaddumi ilayk

I ask You, Oh Allah, a speaking tongue, truthful speech, fitting understanding, savored secret, accepting heart, comprehending intellect, illumined thought, amazed gaze, agitated longing, burning desire and overwhelming ecstasy and grant me an able hand, subduing power, protective eye, content soul, and limbs that do not wane in Your Obedience. Sanctify me as one who is fit to journey towards You and sustain me with the ability to come to You.

إِلَهِي هَبْ لِي قَلْباً أُقْبِلُ بِهِ عَلَيْكَ فِي فَقْرِ الفُقَرَاءِ فَقِيراً، يَقُودُهُ الشَّوْقُ وَيَسُوقُهُ التَّوْقُ إِلَيْكَ، زَادُهُ الخَوْفُ وَرَفِيقُهُ القَلَقُ وَقَصْدُهُ القُرْبُ وَالقَبُولُ وَعِنْدَكَ زُلْفَى القَاصِدِينَ وَمُنْتَهَى رَغْبَةِ الطَّالِبِينَ

Ilāhī hab lī qalban uqbilu bihi ʿalayka fī faqri-l-fuqarāʾi faqīrā, yaqūduhu-sh-shawqu wa yasūquhu-t-tawqu ilayk, zāduhu-l-khawfu wa rafīquhu-l-qalaqu wa qaṣduhu-l-qurbu wa-l-qabūl wa ʿindaka zulfa-l-qāṣidīna wa muntahā raghbati-ṭ-ṭālibīn

Oh Allah, grant me a heart, humble among those who are humble, through which I can enter upon You. Let it be driven by longing, guided by desire for You. Let its sustenance be fear, its companion [blissful] agitation, and its intention nearness and acceptance. With You rests the goal of those with intention and utmost desire of seekers.

إِلَهِي أَلْقِ عَلَيَّ السَّكِينَةَ وَالوَقَارَ وَجَنِّبْنِي العَظَمَةَ وَالاسْتِكْبَارَ وَأَقِمْنِي فِي مَقَامِ القَبُولِ وَالإِنَابَةِ وَقَابِلْ دُعَائِيَ بِالإِجَابَةِ، إِلَهِي قَرِّبْنِي إِلَيْكَ قُرْبَ العَارِفِينَ

Ilāhī alqi ʿalayya-s-sakīnata wa-l-waqāra wa jannibni-l-ʿaẓamata wa-l-istikbār wa aqimnī fī maqāmi-l-qabūli wa-l-inābati wa qābil duʿāʾī bi-l-ijābah, ilāhī qarribnī ilayka qurba-l-ʿārifīn

Oh Allah, cast upon me tranquility and regality. Keep me away from self-aggrandizement and pride. Establish me in the station of acceptance and returning to You. Meet my supplications with response. Oh Allah, grant me a nearness to You as that of the gnostics.

وَقَدِّسْنِي عَنْ عَلَائِقِ الطَّبْعِ وَأَزِل عَنْ قَلْبِي عَلَقِ دَمِ الذَّنْبِ لِأَكُونَ مِنَ الْمُتَطَهِّرِينَ يَا رَبَّ الْعَالَمِينْ وَصَلَّى اللهُ عَلَى سَيِّدِنَا مُحَمَّدٍ وَعلى آلِهِ وَصَحْبِهِ أَجْمَعِينَ

wa qaddisnī ʿan ʿalāʾiqi-ṭ-ṭabʿi wa azil ʿan qalbī ʿalaqa dami-dh-dhanbi li-akūna min-al-mutaṭahhirīna yā Rabbal ʿālamīn, wa ṣallā Allāhu ʿalā sayyidinā Muḥammadin wa ʿalā ālihi wa ṣaḥbihi ajmaʿīna wa-l-ḥamdu lillāhi Rabbi-l-ʿĀlamīn

Sanctify me from the traces of human weakness and remove from my heart the leach of sin, so that I become from those who purify themselves, oh Lord of the worlds. May Allah send His Prayers and Salutations upon our master Muhammad ﷺ, his family and companions in their entirety

يَوْمُ الأَحَدْ

Yawmu-l-Aḥad

The Day of Sunday

بِسْمِ اللهِ فَاتِحِ الوُجُودْ، وَالحَمْدُ للهِ مُظْهِرِ كُلِّ مَوْجُودْ، وَلَا إِلَهَ إِلَّا اللهُ تَوْحِيداً مُطْلَقاً عَنْ كَشْفٍ وَشُهُودْ، وَاللهُ أَكْبَرُ مِنْهُ بَدَأَ الأَمْرُ وَإِلَيْهِ يَعُودْ، وَسُبْحَانَ اللهِ، مَا ثَمَّ سِوَاهُ فَيُشْهَدُ وَلَا مَعَهُ غَيْرُهُ مَعْبُودْ.

Bismillāhi Fātiḥi-l-wujūd, wa-l-ḥamdu lillāhi Muẓhiri kulli mawjūd, wa lā ilāha illa-Allāh tawḥīdan muṭlaqan ʿan kashfin wa shuhūd, wa Allāhu Akbaru minhu badaʾa-l-amru wa ilayhi yaʿūd, wa subḥāna Allāh, mā thamma siwāhu fa-yushhadu wa lā maʿahu ghayruhu maʿbūd.

In the Name of Allah: The Opener of existence. *All praise is due to Allah*: The Manifester of every existent thing. *There is no god but Allah*: An absolute unity in unveiling and witnessing. *Allah is Greater*: From Him the affair began and to Him it returns. *May Allah be Glorified*: There is naught but Him to be witnessed nor is there anyone with Him who is worshipped.

وَاحِدٌ أَحَدٌ عَلَى مَا كَانَ عَلَيْهِ قَبْلَ حُدُوثِ الحُدُودْ. لَهُ فِي كُلِّ شَيْءٍ آيَةٌ تَدُلُّ عَلَى أَنَّهُ وَاحِدٌ أَحَدٌ مَوْجُودْ. سِرُّهُ سَتَرَهُ عَنِ الإِدْرَاكِ وَالنُّفُوذْ. وَلَا حَوْلَ وَلَا قُوَّةَ إِلَّا بِاللهِ العَلِيِّ العَظِيمِ كَنْزٌ اخْتَصَّنَا بِهِ مِنْ خَزَائِنِ الغَيْبِ وَالجُودْ.

Wāḥidun Aḥadun ʿalā mā kāna ʿalayhi qabla ḥudūthi-l-ḥudūd. lahu fī kulli shayʾin āyatun tadullu ʿalā annahu

Wāḥidun Aḥadun Mawjūd. Sirrahu satarahu ʿani-l-idrāki wa-n-nufūd. wa lā ḥawla wa lā quwwata illā billāh al-ʿAliyyi-l-ʿAẓīm kanzun ikhtaṣṣanā bihi min khazāʾini-l-ghaybi wa-l-jūd.

One and Singular, as He was before the emergence of boundaries. In all things there is a sign that points to the fact that He is One, Singular and Being. His Secret He hid from comprehension and dissipation. *There is neither power nor means save through Allah, the Loftiest and Greatest* is a treasure, which He specified for us from the treasuries of the unseen and munificence.

اَسْتَنْزِلُ بِهِ كُلَّ خَيْرٍ وَادْفَعُ بِهِ كُلَّ شَرٍّ وَأَفْتَقُ بِهِ كُلَّ رَتْقٍ مَسْدُودٍ. وَإِنَّا لِلَّهِ وَإِنَّا إِلَيْهِ رَاجِعُونَ فِي كُلِّ أَمْرٍ نَزَلَ أَوْ هُوَ نَازِلٌ وَفِي كُلِّ حَالٍ وَمَقَامٍ وَخَاطِرٍ وَوَارِدٍ وَمَصْدَرٍ وَوُرُودٍ. وَاللهُ هُوَ الْمَرْجُوُّ لِكُلِّ شَيْءٍ وَفِي كُلِّ شَيْءٍ هُوَ الْمَأْمُولُ وَالْمَقْصُودُ.

astanzilu bihi kulla khayrin wa adfaʿu bihi kulla sharrin wa aftaqu bihi kulla ratqin masdūd. wa innā lillāhi wa innā ilayhi rājiʿūna fī kulli amrin nazala aw huwa nāzilun wa fī kulli ḥālin wa maqāmin wa khāṭirin wa wāridin wa maṣdarin wa wurūd. wa Allāhu huwa-l-Marjū li-kulli shayʾin wa fī kulli shayʾin huwa-l-Maʾmūlu wa-l-Maqṣūd.

I call forth, through it[39], every goodness, repel every evil and open forth every closed path. *To Allah we belong and to Him we are returning* in every affair that did or is descending, and in every state, station,

---

[39] In reference to the *ḥayqala*: *lā ḥawla wa lā quwwata illā billāh*

thought, spiritual arrival, source, and advent. Allah is the One who is desired for everything, and in everything He is the Hope and Destination.

الإِلْهَامُ مِنْهُ وَالْفَهْمُ عَنْهُ وَالْمَوْجُودُ هُوَ فَلَا إِنْكَارَ وَلَا جُحُودْ. إِذَا كَشَفَ فَلَا غَيْرٌ وَإِذَا سَتَرَ فَكُلٌّ غَيْرٌ وَالْكُلُّ مَحْجُوبٌ مَبْعُودْ. بَاطِنٌ بِالْأَحَدِيَّةِ ظَاهِرٌ بِالْوَاحِدِيَّةِ وَعَنْهُ وَبِهِ كَوْنُ كُلِّ شَيْءٍ فَلَا شَيْءَ إِذِ الشَّيْءُ فِي الْحَقِيقَةِ مَعْدُومٌ مَفْقُودْ.

al-ilhāmu minhu wa-l-fahmu ʿanhu wa-l-Mawjūdu Huwa fa-lā inkāra wa-lā juḥūd. idhā kashafa fa-lā ghayrun wa idhā satara fa-kullun ghayrun wa-l-kullu maḥjūbun mabʿūd. Bāṭinun bi-l-aḥadiyyati Ẓāhirun bi-l-wāḥidiyyati wa ʿanhu wa bihi kawnu kulli shayʾin fa-lā shayʾa idhi-sh-shayʾu fi-l-ḥaqīqati maʿdūmun mafqūd.

Inspiration is from Him, understanding through Him, Being is He, whence there is no denial nor disavowal. If He unveils, there is no other, yet if He hides, all is another, veiled and distanced. He is Inward in His Singularity and Outward in His Oneness. From and through Him is the existence of everything. Thus, there is nothing. For the thing is non-existent and missing.

فَهُوَ الْأَوَّلُ وَالْآخِرُ وَالظَّاهِرُ وَالْبَاطِنُ وَهُوَ بِكُلِّ شَيْءٍ عَلِيمٌ، قَبْلَ كَوْنِ الشَّيْءِ وَبَعْدَ الْوُجُودْ. لَهُ الْإِحَاطَةُ الْوَاسِعَةُ وَالْحَقِيقَةُ الْجَامِعَةُ

وَالسِّرُّ القَائِمُ وَالمُلْكُ الدَّائِمُ وَالحُكْمُ اللَّازِمْ.

fa-Huwa-l-Awwalu wa-l-Ākhiru wa-ẓ-Ẓāhiru wa-l-Bāṭinu wa Huwa bi-kulli shayʾin ʿAlīm. qabla kawni-sh-shayʾi wa baʿda-l-wujūd. lahu-l-iḥāṭatu-l-wāsiʿatu wa-l-ḥaqīqatu-l-jāmiʿatu wa-s-sirru-l-qāʾimu wa-l-mulku-d-dāʾimu wa-l-ḥukmu-l-lāzim.

He is the First, Last, Outward, Inward and He is Knowledgeable of all things, before and after their existence. To Him belongs the vast envelopment, encompassing reality, attentive secret, continuous dominion, and abiding rule.

أَهْلُ الثَّنَاءِ وَالمَجْدِ هُوَ كَمَا أَثْنَى عَلَى نَفْسِهِ فَهُوَ الحَامِدُ وَالمَحْمُودْ. أَحَدِيُّ الذَّاتِ وَاحِدِيُّ الأَسْمَاءِ وَالصِّفَاتْ. عَلِيمٌ بِالكُلِّيَّاتِ وَالجُزْئِيَّاتْ. مُحِيطٌ بِالفَوْقِيَّاتِ وَالتَّحْتِيَّاتِ وَلَهُ عَنَتِ الوُجُوهُ مِنْ كُلِّ الجِهَاتْ.

Ahlu-th-thanāʾi wa-l-Majdi Huwa ka-mā athnā ʿalā nafsihi fa-Huwa-l-Ḥāmidu wa-l-Maḥmūd. Aḥadiyyu-dh-Dhāti Wāḥidiyyu-l-Asmāʾi wa-ṣ-Ṣifāt. ʿAlīmun bi-l-kulliyyāti wa-l-juzʾiyyat. Muḥīṭun bi-l-fawqiyyāti wa-t-taḥtiyyāti wa lahu ʿanati-l-wujūhu min kulli-l-jihāt.

He is Most Worthy of Praise and Exaltation, as He Praised Himself. Thus, He is the One who Praises and is Praised. Singular in His Essence, One in His Names and Attributes. Fully Knowledgeable of the wholes and parts. Enveloping what is above and below, and to Him are humbled faces from all directions.

اللَّهُمَّ يَا مَنْ هُوَ الْمُحِيطُ الْجَامِعُ وَيَا مَنْ لَا يَمْنَعُهُ عَنِ الْعَطَاءِ مَانِعٌ وَيَا مَنْ لَا يَنْفَدُ مَا عِنْدَهُ وَعَمَّ جَمِيعَ الْخَلَائِقِ جُودُهُ وَرِفْقُهُ، اللَّهُمَّ افْتَحْ لِي أَغْلَاقَ هَذِهِ الْكُنُوزِ وَاكْشِفْ لِي حَقَائِقَ هَذِهِ الرُّمُوزِ.

Allāhumma yā man Huwa-l-Muḥīṭu-l-Jāmiʿu wa yā man lā yamnaʿuhu ʿani-l-ʿaṭāʾi māniʿun wa yā man lā yanfadu mā ʿindahu wa ʿamma jamīʿa-l-khalāʾiqi jūduhu wa rifquh, Allāhumma iftaḥ lī aghlāqa hādhihi-l-kunūz wa-kshif lī ḥaqāʾiqa hādhihi-r-rumūz.

Oh Allah, You who surrounds all and is All-Encompassing, who is hindered by nothing from giving. You whose bounties never expire and whose munificence and kindness permeates all creation; oh Allah, open for me the locks of these treasures and unveil for me the realities of these symbols.

وَكُنْ اللَّهُمَّ مُوَاجِهِي وَوُجْهَتِي وَاحْجُبْنِي بِرُؤْيَتِكَ عَنْ رُؤْيَتِي وَامْحُ بِنُورِ تَجَلِّيكَ جَمِيعَ صِفَتِي حَتَّى لَا يَكُونَ لِي وُجْهَةٌ إِلَّا إِلَيْكَ. انْظُرْ إِلَيَّ بِعَيْنِ الرَّحْمَةِ وَالْعِنَايَةِ وَالْحِفْظِ وَالرِّعَايَةِ وَالِاخْتِصَاصِ وَالْوَلَايَةِ فِي كُلِّ شَيْءٍ

wa kun Allāhumma muwājihī wa wujhatī wa-ḥjubnī bi-ruʾyatika ʿan ruʾyatī wa-mḥu bi-nūri tajallīka jamīʿa ṣifatī ḥattā lā yakūna lī wujhatun illā ilayk. unẓur ilayya bi-ʿayni-r-raḥmati wa-l-ʿināyati wa-l-ḥifẓi wa-r-riʿāyati wa-l-ikhtiṣāṣi wa-l-walāyati fī kulli shayʾ

And be, oh Allah, my direction, destination, and veil

me, through Your perception, from my vision. Erase through the light of Your Manifestation my entire attribute, so that I can have no direction except towards You. Gaze upon me with the eye/essence/spring[40] of mercy, attention, protection, care, advantage, and sainthood in all things.

حَتَّى لَا يَحْجُبُنِي عَنْ رُؤْيَتِي لَكَ شَيْءٌ وَأَكُونَ نَاظِراً إِلَيْكَ بِمَا أَمْدَدْتَنِي بِهِ مِنْ نَظَرِكَ فِي كُلِّ شَيْءٍ. وَاجْعَلْنِي خَاضِعاً لِتَجَلِّيكَ أَهْلاً لِاخْتِصَاصِكَ وَتَوَلِّيكَ مَحَلًّا لِنَظَرِكَ مِنْ خَلْقِكَ مُفِيضاً عَلَيْهِمْ مِنْ عَطَائِكَ وَفَضْلِكَ.

ḥattā lā yaḥjubunī ʿan ruʾyatī laka shayʾun wa akūna nāẓiran ilayka bi-mā amdadtanī bihi min naẓarika fī kulli shayʾ. wa-jʿalnī khāḍiʿan li-tajallīka ahlan li-khtiṣāṣika wa tawallīka maḥallan li-naẓarika min khalqika mufīḍan ʿalayhim min ʿaṭāʾika wa faḍlik.

So that I am not veiled from seeing You by anything, and I can perceive You through what You have sustained me with, through Your own perception of all things. Make me submit always to Your Manifestation, be fit for Your Designation and Guardianship, under Your Gaze among creation, whereby I can bestow upon them from Your Bounties and Grace.

---

[40] The word *ʿayn*, as utilized by Shaykh al-Akbar and many other Sufi masters often denotes, at least, three meanings all at once: eye, essence and/or spring.

يَا مَنْ لَهُ الغِنَا الْمُطْلَقُ وَلِعَبْدِهِ الفَقْرُ الْمُحَقَّقُ. يَا غَنِيٌّ عَنْ كُلِّ شَيْءٍ وَكُلُّ شَيْءٍ مُفْتَقِرٌ إِلَيْهِ. يَا مَنْ بِيَدِهِ أَمْرُ كُلِّ شَيْءٍ وَكُلُّ شَيْءٍ رَاجِعٌ إِلَيْهِ. يَا مَنْ لَهُ الْوُجُودُ الْمُطْلَقُ فَلَا يَعْلَمُ مَا هُوَ إِلَّا هُوَ وَلَا يُسْتَدَلُّ عَلَيْهِ إِلَّا بِهِ.

yā man lahu-l-Ghinā al-Muṭlaq wa li-ʿabdihi-l-faqru-l-muḥaqqaq. yā Ghaniyyun ʿan kulli shayʾin wa kullu shayʾin muftaqirun ilayh. yā man bi-yadihi amru kulli shayʾin wa kullu shayʾin rājiʿun ilayh. yā man lahu-l-Wujūdu-l-Muṭlaqu fa-lā yaʿlamu mā Huwa illā Huwa wa lā yustadallu ʿalayhi illā bih.

You, to whom belongs Absolute Sufficiency and to whose servant belongs realized impoverishment. You, who is Independent from all things, yet upon Whom everything is dependent. You, in whose Hands are the affairs of all things, and to You they return. You, to whom belongs Absolute Being, and who cannot be known save by You, and only through You can You be found.

وَيَا مُسَخِّرَ الْأَعْمَالَ الصَّالِحَةَ لِلْعَبْدِ لِيَعُودَ نَفْعُهَا عَلَيْهِ. لَا مَقْصَدَ لِي غَيْرُكَ وَلَا يَسَعُنِي إِلَّا جُودُكَ وَخَيْرُكَ. يَا جَوَادُ فَوْقَ الْمُرَادِ وَيَا مُعْطِيَ النَّوَالَ قَبْلَ السُّؤَالْ. يَا مَنْ وَقَفَ دُونَهُ قَدْمُ عَقْلِ كُلِّ طَالِبْ.

wa yā Musakhkhira-l-aʿmāla-ṣ-ṣāliḥata li-l-ʿabdi li-yaʿūda nafʿuhā ʿalayh. lā maqṣada lī ghayruka wa lā yasaʿunī illā jūduka wa khayruk. yā Jawādu fawqa-l-murādi wa yā

Muʿṭiya-n-nawāla qabla-s-suʾāl. yā man waqafa dūnahu qudmu ʿaqli kulli ṭālib.

You, who subjects righteous deeds for the servant so that their benefits return to him, I have no intention other than You, nor can I be satisfied with other than Your Munificence and Goodness. Oh, Most Generous beyond our ambition, and He who grants what is desired before it is sought. You, before whom the courageous intellect of every seeker halts.

يَا مَنْ هُوَ عَلَى أَمْرِهِ قَادِرٌ وَغَالِبٌ، يَا مَنْ هُوَ لِكُلِّ شَيْءٍ وَاهِبٌ وَإِذَا شَاءَ سَالِبْ، أَهُمُّ بِالسُّؤَالِ إِلَيْكَ فَأَجِدْنِيَ عَبْدًا لَكَ عَلَى كُلِّ حَالْ. فَتَوَلَّنِيَ يَا مَوْلَايَ فَأَنْتَ أَوْلَى بِي مِنِّي.

yā man Huwa ʿalā amrihi Qādirun wa Ghālib, yā man Huwa li-kulli shayʾin Wāhibun wa idhā shāʾa Sālib, ahummu bi-s-suʾāli ilayka faʾajidnī ʿabdan laka ʿalā kulli ḥāl. fa-tawallanī yā Mawlāya fa-anta awlā bī minnī.

Oh You, who is All Powerful and Able to execute His Commands. Oh, You who Grants all things and if He wills, Deprives. I turn to you with my needs, so found me a servant for You in every state. Take me under Your Guardianship, oh my Guardian, for You are more deserving, to me, than myself.

كَيْفَ أَقْصِدُكَ وَأَنْتَ وَرَاءَ الْقَصْدْ؟ أَمْ كَيْفَ أَطْلُبُكَ وَالطَّلَبُ عَيْنُ الْبُعْدِ؟ أَيُطْلَبُ مَنْ هُوَ قَرِيبٌ حَاضِرْ؟ أَمْ يُقْصَدُ مَنِ الْقَصْدُ فِيهِ تَائِهُ

وَحَائِرْ؟ الطَّلَبُ لَا يَصِلُ إِلَيْكَ وَالقَصْدُ لَا يَصْدُرُ عَلَيْكْ.

kayfa aqṣiduka wa Anta warāʾa-l-qaṣd? am kayfa aṭlubuka wa-ṭ-ṭalabu ʿaynu-l-buʿd? ayuṭlabu man Huwa Qarībun Ḥāḍir? am yuqṣadu mani-l-qaṣdu fīhi tāʾihun wa ḥāʾir? aṭ-ṭalabu lā yaṣilu ilayka wa-l-qaṣdu lā yaṣduru ʿalayk.

How can I intend You when You are behind the intention? How can I seek You if seeking is the essence of distance? Is He sought, He who is Near and Present? Or is He intended, He within whom intention is lost and perplexed? Our seeking cannot reach you, nor can our intention occur prior to You.

تَجَلِّيَاتُ ظَاهِرِكَ لَا تُلْحَقُ وَلَا تُدْرَكُ وَرُمُوزُ أَسْرَارِكَ لَا تَنْحَلُّ وَلَا تَنفَكْ. أَيَعْلَمُ المَوْجُودُ كُنْهَ مَنْ أَوْجَدَهْ؟ أَمْ يَبْلُغُ العَبْدُ حَقِيقَةَ مَنِ اسْتَعْبَدَهْ؟ الطَّلَبُ وَالقَصْدُ وَالقُرْبُ وَالبُعْدُ مِنْ صِفَاتِ العَبْدْ، فَمَاذَا يُدْرِكُ العَبْدُ بِصِفَاتِهِ مِمَّنْ هُوَ مُنَزَّهٌ مُتَعَالٍ فِي ذَاتِهْ؟

tajalliyātu ẓāhiruka lā tulḥaq wa lā tudrak wa rumūzu asrārika lā tanḥallu wa lā tanfak. ayaʿlamu-l-mawjūdu Kunha man awjadah? am yablughu-l-ʿabdu ḥaqīqata mani-staʿbadah? aṭ-ṭalabu wa-l-qaṣdu wa-l-qurbu wa-l-buʿdu min ṣifāti-l-ʿabd, fa-mādhā yudriku-l-ʿabdu bi-ṣifātihi mimman Huwa Munazzahun Mutaʿālin fī Dhātih?

The Manifestations of Your Outward can neither be surpassed nor comprehended. The symbols of Your Secrets can neither be unknotted nor deciphered. Can the existent thing know the essence of He who found it? Or can the servant reach the reality of the One who put them in servitude? Seeking, intention, nearness and distance are among the traits of the servant, so what can a servant comprehend, with his traits, of He who is Sanctified and Sublime in Essence?

وَكُلُّ مَخْلُوقٍ مَحَلُّهُ العَجْزُ فِي مَوْقِفِ العِزِّ عَنْ نَيْلِ إِدْرَاكِ هَذَا الكَنْزِ. كَيْفَ أَعْرِفُكَ وَأَنْتَ البَاطِنُ الَّذِي لَا تُعْرَفْ؟ وَكَيْفَ لَا أَعْرِفُكَ وَأَنْتَ الظَّاهِرُ الَّذِي إِلَيَّ فِي كُلِّ شَيْءٍ تَتَعَرَّفْ؟

wa kullu makhlūqin maḥalluhu-l-ʿajzu fī mawqifi-l-ʿizzi ʿan nayli idrāki hādha-l-kanz. kayfa aʿrifuka wa anta-l-Bāṭinu al-ladhī lā tuʿraf? wa kayfa lā aʿrifuka wa anta-ẓ-Ẓāhiru al-ladhī ilayya fī kulli shayʾin tataʿarraf?

Every created thing resides in inability, at the altar of exaltedness, from reaching to comprehend this treasure. How can I know You when You are the Inward who cannot be known? Yet, how can I not know You, when You are the Outward who makes Himself known to me through all things?

كَيْفَ أُوَحِّدُكَ وَلَا وُجودَ لِي فِي عَيْنِ الأَحَدِيَّةْ؟ وَكَيْفَ لَا أُوَحِّدُكَ وَالتَّوْحِيدُ سِرُّ العُبُودِيَّةْ؟ سُبْحَانَكَ لَا إِلَهَ إِلَّا أَنْتْ. مَا وَحَّدَكَ مِنْ أَحَدٍ سِوَاكَ إِذْ أَنْتَ كَمَا أَنْتَ فِي سَابِقِ الأَزَلِ وَلَاحِقِ الأَبَدْ.

kayfa uwaḥḥiduka wa lā wujūda lī fī ʿayni-l-ʿaḥadiyyah? wa kayfa lā uwaḥḥiduka wa-t-tawḥīdu sirru-l-ʿubūdiyyah? Subḥānaka lā ilāha illā Ant.

mā waḥḥadaka min aḥadin Siwāka idh anta ka mā anta fī sābiqi-l-azali wa lāḥiqi-l-abad.

How can I declare Your Singularity when I have no existence in the essence of singularity? Yet, how can I not declare Your Singularity when doing so is the secret of servanthood? Glory be to You, there is no god but You. No one has declared Your Singularity save You, for You are as You have been since pre-eternity and until eternity.

فِفِي التَّحْقِيقِ مَا وَحَّدَكَ سِوَاكَ وَفِي الجُمْلَةِ مَا عَرَفَكَ إِلَّا إِيَّاكْ. بَطَنْتَ وَظَهَرْتَ فَلَا عَنْكَ بَطَنْتَ وَلَا لِغَيْرِكَ ظَهَرْت. فَأَنْتَ أَنْتَ لَا إِلَهَ إِلَّا أَنْت. فَكَيْفَ بِهَذَا الشَّكْلِ يَنحَلُّ وَالأَوَّلُ آخِرٌ وَالآخِرُ أَوَّلْ؟

fa-fi-t-taḥqīqi mā waḥḥadaka Siwāka wa fi-l-jumlati mā ʿarafaka illā Iyyāk. Baṭanta wa Ẓaharta fa-lā ʿanka Baṭanta wa lā li-ghayrika Ẓahart. fa-Anta Anta lā ilāha illā Ant. fa kayfa bi-hādha-sh-shakli yanḥallu wa-l-Awwalu Ākhirun wa-l-Ākhiru Awwal?

In reality, no one has declared Your Oneness save You. In actuality, no one has known You save You. You have become Inward and Outward, yet neither from You have you become Inward nor from other than You have you become Outward. You are You, there is no god but You. And so, how can the affair be resolved in this way, when He who is First is Last, and He who is Last is also First?

فَيَا مَنْ أَبْهَمَ الأَمْرَ وَأَبْطَنَ السِّرَ وَأَوْقَعَ الحَيْرَةَ وَلَا غَيْرَهْ. أَسْأَلُكَ

اللهُمَّ كَشفَ سِرِّ الأَحَدِيَّةِ وَتَحْقِيقِ العُبُودِيَّةِ وَالقِيَامُ بِالرُّبُوبِيَّةِ كَمَا يَلِيقُ بِحَضْرَتِهَا العَلِيَّةْ. فَأَنَا مَوْجُودٌ بِكَ حَادِثٌ مَعْدُومْ

fa-yā man Abhama-l-amra wa Abṭana-s-sirra wa Awqaʿa-l-ḥayrata wa lā ghayruh. asʾaluka Allāhumma kashfa sirri-l-aḥadiyyati wa taḥqīqi-l-ʿubūdiyyati wa-l-qiyāmu bi-r-rubūbiyyati ka-mā yalīqu bi-ḥaḍratiha-l-ʿaliyyah. Fa-anā mawjūdun Bika ḥādithun maʿdūm.

Oh You, and only You, who has coded this affair, made the secret inward and caused perplexity to occur; I ask You, oh Allah, to unveil the secret of singularity, realization of servanthood and to establish Lordship as befits its lofty presence, for indeed, I exist through You, yet remain a non-existent accident.

وَأَنْتَ مَوْجُودٌ بَاقٍ حَيٌّ قَيُّومٌ قَدِيمٌ أَزَلِيٌّ عَالِمٌ مَعْلُومْ. فَيَا مَنْ لَا يَعْلَمُ مَا هُوَ إِلَّا هُوَ وَلَا يُسْتَدَلُّ عَلَيْهِ إِلَّا بِهْ. أَسْأَلُكَ الهَرَبَ مِنِّي إِلَيْكَ وَالجَمْعَ بِجَمِيعِ مَجْمُوعِي عَلَيْكَ حَتَّى لَا يَكُونَ وُجُودِي حِجَابِي عَنْ شُهُودِي.

wa Anta Mawjūdun Bāqin Ḥayyun Qayyūmun Qadīmun Azaliyyun ʿĀlimun Maʿlūm. fa yā man lā yaʿlamu mā Huwa illā Huwa wa lā yustadallu ʿalayhi illā bih. asʾaluka-l-haraba minnī ilayka wa-l-jamʿa bi-jamīʿi majmūʿī ʿalayka ḥattā lā yakūna wujūdī ḥijābī ʿan shuhūdī.

While You are Existence, Subsistence, Eternally Living, Everlasting, Before Time and Pre-Eternal, All-

Knowing and Known. Oh You, whom no one can know save You, and only through whom You can be found. I ask You, for me, to flee from myself to You, to gather me in my entirety upon You so that my being does not become my veil from witnessing You.

يَا مَقْصُودِي يَا مَعْبُودِي، مَا فَاتَنِي شَيْءٌ إِذَا أَنَا وَجَدْتُكَ وَلَا جَهِلْتُ شَيْئاً إِذَا أَنَا عَلِمْتُكَ وَلَا قَصَدْتُ شَيْئاً إِذَا أَنَا شَهِدْتُكْ. فَنَائِي فِيكَ وَبَقَائِي بِكَ وَمَشْهُودِيَ أَنْتْ.

yā maqṣūdī yā maʿbūdī, mā fātanī shayʾun idhā anā wajadtuka wa lā jahiltu shayʾan idhā anā ʿalimtuka wa lā qaṣadtu shayʾan idhā anā shahidtuk. fanāʾī fīka wa baqāʾī bika wa mashhūdī Ant.

Oh You, my intention and the One I worship, nothing has passed me if I find You nor have I become ignorant of anything if I know You, nor have I intended anything else if I witness You. My annihilation is in You, subsistence through You and You are whom I witness.

أَنْتَ كَمَا شَهِدْتَ وَكَمَا أَمَرْتَ فَشُهودِيَ عَيْنُ وُجودِي. فَمَا شَهِدْتُ سِوَائِي فِي فَنَائِي وَبَقَائِي فَالإِشَارَةُ إِلَيَّ وَالحُكْمُ لِي وَعَلَيَّ وَالنِّسْبَةُ نِسْبَتِي وَكُلُّ ذَلِكَ رُتْبَتِي وَالشَّأْنُ شَأْنِي فِي الظُّهُورِ وَالبُطُونِ وَسَرَيَانِ السِّرِ المَصُونْ.

Anta ka-mā shahidta wa ka-mā amarta fa-shuhūdī ʿaynu

wujūdī. fa-mā shahidtu siwāʾī fī fanāʾī wa baqāʾī fa-l-ishāratu ilayya wa-l-ḥukmu lī wa ʿalayya wa-n-nisbatu nisbatī wa kullu dhālika rutbatī wa-sh-shaʾnu shaʾnī fi-ẓ-ẓuhūri wa-l-buṭūni wa sarayāni-s-sirri-l-maṣūn.

You are as You have Witnessed and Commanded. Thus, my witnessing is the essence of my own existence. I have not witnessed other than myself in my annihilation and subsistence. The allusion is towards me, the ruling for and upon me, and the relationship is mine. All of this is my rank and affair, in appearance, hiding and the permeation of the preserved secret.

هُوِيَّةٌ سَارِيَةٌ مَظَاهِرُ بَادِيَةٌ وُجودٌ وَعَدَمٌ نُورٌ وَظُلَمٌ سَمْعٌ وَصَمَمٌ لَوْحٌ وَقَلَمٌ جَهْلٌ وَعِلْمٌ حَرْبٌ وَسِلْمٌ صَمْتٌ وَنُطْقٌ رَتْقٌ وَفَتْقٌ حَقِيقَةٌ وَحَقٌّ غَيْبُوبِيَّةُ أَزَلٍ وَدَيْمُومِيَّةُ أَبَدْ.

Huwiyyatun Sāriyatun maẓāhirun bādiyatun wujūdun wa ʿadamun nūrun wa ẓulamun samʿun wa ṣamamun lawḥun wa qalamun jahlun wa ʿilmun ḥarbun wa silmun ṣamtun wa nuṭqun ratqun wa fatqun ḥaqīqatun wa ḥaqqun ghaybūbiyyatu azalin wa daymūmiyyatu abad.

A Permeating Divine Identity, unique appearances, existence and non-existence, light and darknesses, hearing and deafness, tablet and pen, ignorance and knowledge, war and peace, silence and utterance, closure and opening, reality and truth, a pre-eternal unseen and eternal continuity.

﴿قُلْ هُوَ اللهُ أَحَدٌ ۞ اللهُ الصَّمَدُ ۞ لَمْ يَلِدْ وَلَمْ يُولَدْ ۞ وَلَمْ يَكُن لَّهُ كُفُوًا أَحَدٌ﴾ وَصَلَّى اللهُ عَلَى الأَوَّلِ فِي الإِيجَادِ وَالوُجودِ وَالفَاتِحِ لِكُلِّ شَاهِدٍ وَمَشْهُودْ. السِّرِ البَاطِنِ وَالنُّورِ الظَّاهِرْ.

"Qul Huwa-l-Allāhu Aḥad. Allāhu-ṣ-Ṣamad. Lam Yalid wa lam Yūlad. Wa lam yaku-l-lahu kufuwan aḥad" wa ṣallā Allāhu ʿala-l-awwali fi-l-ījādi wa-l-wujūdi wa-l-fātiḥi li-kulli shāhidin wa mashhūd. as-sirri-l-bāṭini wa-n-nūri-ẓ-ẓāhir.

"Say: 'He is Allah the Singular. Allah the Self-Sufficient. He neither gave birth nor was He born. Nor is anyone comparable to Him." And may Allah send His Prayers upon the first in creation and existence. The opener for every witnesser and witnessed thing. The inward secret and outward light.

عَيْنِ المَقْصودِ مُمَيَّزِ قَصَبِ السَّبْقِ فِي عَالَمِ الخَلْقِ فِي المَخْصُوصِ وَالمَعْبُودْ. الرُّوحِ الأَقْدَسِ العَلِيِّ وَالنورِ الأَكْمَلِ البَهِيّ. القَائِمِ بِكَمَالِ العُبُودِيَّةِ فِي المَعْبُودْ. الَّذِي أُفِيضَ عَلَى رُوحِي مِنْ حَضْرَةِ رُوحَانِيَّتِهْ

ʿayni-l-maqṣūdi qaṣabi-s-sabqi fī ʿālami-l-khalqi fi-l-makhṣūṣi wa-l-maʿbūd. ar-rūḥi-l-aqdasi-l-ʿaliyyi wa-n-nūri-l-akmali-l-bahiyy. al-qāʾimi bi-kamāli-l-ʿubūdiyyati fi-l-maʿbūd. al-ladhī ufīḍa ʿalā rūḥī min ḥaḍrati rūḥāniyyatih

The essence of intention, the distinguished preordained golden threads in the realm of creation, elite and worshipped. The lofty most-sanctified spirit and lustrous perfected light. The servant who embodies the perfect servanthood. He from whose spiritual presence has flowed forth upon my spirit.

وَاتَّصَلَتْ بِمِشْكَاةِ قَلْبِي أَشِعَّةُ نُورَانِيَّتِهْ. فَهُوَ الرَّسُولُ الأَعْظَمُ وَالنَّبِيُّ الْمُكْرَمُ وَالوَلِيُّ الْمُقَرَّبُ الْمَسْعُودْ. وَعَلَى آلِهِ وَأَصْحَابِهِ خَزَائِنِ أَسْرَارِهِ وَمَطَالِعِ أَنْوَارِهْ. كُنُوزِ الحَقَائِقِ وَهُدَاةِ الخَلَائِقْ. نُجُومِ الهُدَى لِمَنْ اقْتَدَى.

wa-t-taṣalat bi-mishkāti qalbī ashiʿʿatu nūrāniyyatih. fa-huwa-r-rasūlu-l-aʿẓam wa-n-nabiyyu-l-mukramu wa-l-waliyyu-l-muqarrabu-l-masʿūd. wa ʿalā ālihi wa aṣḥābihi khazāʾini asrārihi wa maṭāliʿi anwārih. kunūzi-l-ḥaqāʾiqi wa hudāti-l-khalaʾiq. nujūmi-l-hudā li-mani-qtadā.

And whose rays of illumination connected with the niche of my heart. Indeed, he is the greatest messenger, honored prophet and guardian brought near and made joyous. And upon his family and companions, the treasuries of his secrets, rising places of his lights. The treasures of realities and guides of creation. The stars of guidance for the one who follows them.

وَسَلِّمْ تَسْلِيمًا كَثِيرًا إِلَى يَوْمِ الدِّينْ. وَسُبْحَانَ اللهِ وَمَا أَنَا مِنَ الْمُشْرِكِينْ. حَسْبِيَ اللهُ وَنِعْمَ الوَكِيلْ وَلَا حَوْلَ وَلَا قُوَّةَ إِلَّا بِاللهِ العَلِيِّ العَظِيمْ، وَالحَمْدُ للهِ رَبِّ العَالَمِينْ.

wa sallim taslīman kathīran ilā yawmi-d-dīn. wa Subḥānallāhi wa mā anā mina-l-mushrikīn. ḥasbiya Allāhu wa niʿma-l-wakīl wa lā ḥawla wa lā quwwata illā billāh al-ʿAliyyi-l-ʿAẓīm, wa-l-ḥamdu lillāhi Rabbil ʿĀlamīn.

And send abundant salutations until the Day of Judgment. All Glory belongs to Allah, and I am not from the polytheists. Allah is sufficient for me, and He is the best of patrons. Indeed, there is neither means nor power save through Allah, the Most Lofty and Greatest. All Praise is due to Allah the Lord of the Worlds.

لَيْلَةُ الإِثْنَيْن

Laylatu-l-Ithnayn

The Night of Monday

إِلَهِي وَسِعَ عِلْمُكَ كُلَّ مَعْلُومٍ وَأَحَاطَتْ خِبْرَتُكَ بِبَاطِنِ كُلِّ مَفْهُومٍ وَتَقَدَّسْتَ فِي عُلاكَ عَنْ كُلِّ مَذْمُومْ. تَسَامَتْ إِلَيْكَ الهِمَمُ وَصَعَدَ إِلَيْكَ الكَلِمُ وَأَنْتَ المُتَعَالِي فِي سُمُوِّكَ فَأَقْرَبُ مَعَارِجِنَا إِلَيْكَ التَّنَزُّلُ وَأَنْتَ المُتَعَزِّزُ فِي عُلُوِّكَ فَأَشْرَفُ أَخْلاقِنَا إِلَيْكَ التَّذَلُّلْ.

Ilāhī wasi'a 'ilmuka kulla ma'lūmin wa aḥāṭat khibratuka bi-bāṭini kulli mafhūmin wa taqaddasta fī 'ulāka 'an kulli madhmūm. tasāmat ilayka-l-himamu wa ṣa'ada ilayka-l-kalimu wa Anta-l-Muta'ālī fī sumuwwika fa-aqrabu ma'ārijinā ilayka-t-tanazzulu wa anta-l-muta'azzizu fī 'uluwwika fa-ashrafu akhlāqinā ilayka-t-tadhallul.

Oh Allah, Your Knowledge has encompassed every known thing, and Your Awareness has surrounded the inward of every understood thing. You are Sanctified in Your Loftiness, from every lowly trait. Ambitions elevate to You; Words ascend to you while You are the Loftiest in Your Elevation. Hence, our nearest ascension to You is [Your] Descent [to us]. You are the Most Exalted in Your Loftiness. Hence, humility is our most honorable manners towards You.

ظَهَرْتَ فِي كُلِّ بَاطِنٍ وَظَاهِرٍ وَدُمْتَ بَعْدَ كُلِّ أَوَّلٍ وَآخِرٍ سُبْحَانَكَ لَا إِلَهَ إِلَّا أَنْتَ سَجَدَتْ لِعَظَمَتِكَ الجِبَاهُ وَتَنَعَّمَتْ بِذِكْرِكَ الشِّفَاهْ

أَسْأَلُكَ بِإِسْمِكَ الَّذِي إِلَيْهِ سُمُوُّ كُلِّ مُتَرَقٍّ وَمِنْهُ قَبُولِ كُلِّ مُتَلَقٍّ سِرًّا تَطْلُبُنِي فِيهِ الهِمَمُ العَلِيَّةُ وَتَنْقَادُ إِلَيَّ فِيهِ النُّفُوسُ الأَبِيَّةْ.

ẓaharta fī kulli bāṭinin wa ẓāhirin wa dumta baʿda kulli awwalin wa ākhirin subḥānaka lā ilāha illā Anta sajadat li-ʿaẓamatika-l-jibāhu wa tanaʿʿamat bi-dhikrika-sh-shifāh. as'aluka bi-Ismika al-ladhī ilayhi sumuwwi kulli mutaraqqin wa minhu qabūli kulli mutalaqqin sirran taṭlubunī fīhi-l-himamu-l-ʿaliyyatu wa tanqādu ilayya fīhi-n-nufūsu-l-abiyyah.

You have Appeared in every inward and outward, and Subsisted after every first and last. Glory be to You, there is no god but You. Foreheads prostrate to Your Greatness, and tongues find bounty in Your Remembrance. I ask You, through Your Name, to which elevates every ascender, and from which is the acceptance of every receiver, a secret through which lofty ambitions seek me and stubborn souls follow me.

وَأَسْأَلُكَ رَبِّ أَنْ تَجْعَلَ سُلَّمِي إِلَيْكَ التَّنَزُّلُ وَمِعْرَاجِي إِلَيْكَ التَّخَضُّعُ وَالتَّذَلُّلْ. وَاكْفِنِي بِغَاشِيَةٍ مِنْ نُورِكَ تَكْشِفُ لِي عَنْ كُلِّ مَستُورٍ وَتَحْجُبُنِي عَنْ كُلِّ حَاسِدٍ مَغْرُورٍ وَهَبْ لِي خُلُقًا أَسَعُ بِهِ كُلَّ خَلْقٍ وَاقْضِي بِهِ كُلَّ حَقٍّ كَمَا وَسِعْتَ كُلَّ شَيْءٍ رَحْمَةً وَعِلْمًا يَا رَحْمٰنُ يَا رَحِيمْ

wa as'aluka Rabbī an tajʿala sullamī ilayka-t-tanazzulu wa miʿrājī ilayka-t-takhaḍḍuʿu wa-t-tadhallul. wa-kfinī bi-ghāshiyatin min Nūrika takshifu lī ʿan kulli mastūrin wa taḥjubunī ʿan kulli ḥāsidin maghrūrin wa hab lī khuluqan asaʿu bihi kulla khalqin wa aqḍī bihi kulla ḥaqqin ka-mā wasiʿta kulla shayʾin raḥmatan wa ʿilman yā Raḥmānu yā Raḥīm.

I ask You, oh my Lord, that You make my steps to You [Your] descent [to me] and my ascension to You [my] submission and humility. Suffice me with a curtain from Your Light to unveil for me every hidden thing and hide me from every arrogant and envious person. Grant me a trait through which I may envelop every created thing and fulfill every right, as You have encompassed everything in mercy and knowledge, oh Most Merciful and Beneficent.

لَا إِلَهَ إِلَّا أَنْتَ يَا حَيُّ يَا قَيُّومُ ﴿اللهُ لَا إِلَهَ إِلَّا هُوَ الْحَيُّ الْقَيُّومُ لَا تَأْخُذُهُ سِنَةٌ وَلَا نَوْمٌ لَهُ مَا فِي السَّمَوٰتِ وَمَا فِي الْأَرْضِ مَنْ ذَا الَّذِي يَشْفَعُ عِنْدَهُ إِلَّا بِإِذْنِهِ يَعْلَمُ مَا بَيْنَ أَيْدِيهِمْ وَمَا خَلْفَهُمْ وَلَا يُحِيطُونَ بِشَيْءٍ مِنْ عِلْمِهِ إِلَّا بِمَا شَاءَ وَسِعَ كُرْسِيُّهُ السَّمَوٰتِ وَالْأَرْضَ وَلَا يَؤُودُهُ حِفْظُهُمَا وَهُوَ الْعَلِيُّ الْعَظِيمُ﴾[41]

lā ilāha illā Anta yā Ḥayyu yā Qayyūmu "Allāhu lā ilāha illā Huwa-l-Ḥayyu-l-Qayyūmu lā taʾkhudhuhu sinatu-w-wa lā nawmu-l-lahu mā fi-s-samāwāti wa mā fi-l-arḍi man dha-l-ladhī yashfaʿu ʿindahu illā bi-idhnihi yaʿlamu mā

---

[41] البقرة 255

bayna aydīhim wa mā khalfihum wa lā yuḥīṭūna bi-shay'i-m-min 'Ilmihi illā bi-mā shā'a wasi'a kursiyyuhu-s-samāwāti wa-l-arḍa wa lā ya'ūduhu ḥifẓuhumā wa Huwa-l-'Aliyyu-l-'Aẓīm"

There is no god but You oh Eternally Living and Self-Standing "Allah there is no god but He, the Eternally Living and Self-Standing, neither slumber nor sleep overtakes Him. To Him belongs all that is in the heavens and earth. Who can intercede in His Presence save by His permission. He knows what is between their hands and behind them, and they do not encompass of His Knowledge save what He wills. His throne encompasses the heavens and earth and guarding them does not tire Him. He is the Most Lofty and Greatest"

رَبِّ رَبِّنِي بِلَطِيفِ رُبُوبِيَّتِكَ تَرْبِيَةَ مُفْتَقِرٍ إِلَيْكَ لَا يَسْتَغْنِي عَنْكَ أَبَدًا وَرَاقِبْنِي بِعَيْنِ عِنَايَتِكَ بُمَرَاقَبَةٍ تَحْفَظُنِي مِنْ كُلِّ طَارِقٍ يَطْرُقُنِي بِسُوءٍ فِي نَفْسِي أَوْ يُكَدِّرُ عَلَيَّ وَقْتِي وَحِينِي وَأَثْبِتْ فِي لَوْحِ إِرَادَتِي حَظَّ حَظٍّ يُوصِلُنِي إِلَيْكَ

Rabbi rabbinī bi-laṭīfi rubūbiyyatika tarbiyata muftaqirin ilayka lā yastaghnī 'anka abadan wa rāqibnī bi-'ayni 'ināyatika bi-murāqabatin taḥfaẓunī min kulli ṭāriqin yaṭruqunī bi-sū'in fī nafsī aw yukaddiru 'alayya waqtī wa ḥīnī wa athbit fī lawḥi irādatī ḥaẓẓa ḥaẓẓin yūṣilunī ilayka

Oh, my Lord, care for me with the gentleness of Your Lordship, the care for one who needs You and can never be independent of you. Elevate me, through the essence of Your Attentiveness and a guardianship that protects me from everything that comes towards me with evil or dilutes my time and state. Establish in the tablet of my will a fortunate share to deliver me to You

وَاسْعِدْنِي بِجِدٍّ سَعِيدٍ يُسعِفُنِي إِلَيكَ وَارْزُقْنِي رَاحَةَ الأُنْسِ بِكَ وَرَقِّنِي إِلَى مَقَامِ القُرْبِ مِنْكَ وَرَوِّحْ رُوحِي بِذِكْرِكَ وَرَدِّنِي بِرِدَاءِ الرِّضْوَانِ وَاوْرِدْنِي مَوَارِدَ القَبُولِ وَهَبْ لِي رَحْمَةً مِنْكَ تَلُمُّ شَعَثِي وَتُكْمِلُ نَقْصِي وَتُقَوِّمُ عِوَجِي وَتَرُدُّ شَارِدِي وَتَهْدِي حَائِرِي فَإِنَّكَ رَبُّ كُلِّ شَيءٍ وَمُرَبِّيهْ.

wa asʿidnī bi-jiddin saʿīdin yusʿifunī ilayka wa-rzuqnī rāḥata-l-unsi bika wa raqqinī ilā maqāmi-l-qurbi minka wa rawwiḥ rūḥī bi-dhikrika wa raddinī bi-ridāʾi-r-riḍwāni wa awridnī mawārida-l-qabūli wa hab lī raḥmatan minka talummu shaʿathī wa tukmilu naqṣī wa tuqawwimu ʿiwajī wa taruddu shāridī wa tahdī ḥāʾirī fa-innaka Rabbu kulli shayʾin wa Murabbīh.

Make me joyous with a happy strength that carries me to You. Sustain me with the tranquility of intimacy with You and elevate me to the station of nearness with You. Grant my spirit ease through Your Remembrance. Dress me with the garment of contentment. Open for me the pathways of acceptance and gift me a mercy from You that rectifies my disorientation and guides my perplexity.

Indeed, You are the Lord of everything and its nurturer.

أَنْتَ رَحْمَةُ الذَّوَاتِ وَرَفِيعُ الدَّرَجاتْ. قُرْبُكَ رَوحُ الأَرْوَاحِ وَرَيْحانُ الأَفْرَاحِ وَعُنْوَانُ الفَلاحُ وَرَاحةُ كُلِّ مُرْتَاحْ. تَبَارَكْتَ رَبَّ الأَرْبَابِ وَمُعْتِقَ الرِّقَابِ وَكَاشِفَ العَذَابْ. وَسِعْتَ كُلَّ شَيءٍ رَحْمَةً وَعِلْمًا وَغَفَرْتَ الذُّنُوبَ حَنَانًا وَحِلْمًا وَأَنْتَ الغَفُورُ الرَّحِيمُ الحَلِيمُ العَلِيمُ العَلِيُّ العَظِيمْ.

Anta Raḥmatu-dh-dhawāti wa Rafīʿu-d-Darajāt. qurbuka rawḥu-l-arwāḥi wa rayḥānu-l-afrāḥi wa ʿunwānu-l-falāḥu wa rāḥatu kulli murtāḥ. Tabārakta Rabba-l-arbābi wa Muʿtiqa-r-riqābi wa Kāshifa-l-ʿadhāb. wasiʿta kulla shayʾin raḥmatan wa ʿilman wa ghafarta-dh-dhunūba ḥanānan wa ḥilman wa Anta-l-Ghafūru-r-Raḥīmu-l-Ḥalīmu-l-ʿAlīmu-l-ʿAliyyu-l-ʿAẓīm.

You are the Mercy for essences and Most Lofty in ranks. Nearness to You is the ease of spirits, fragrance of joy, sign of felicity and tranquility of all who are tranquil. May You be Blessed, oh Lord of lords, savior of souls and easer of punishment. You have encompassed all things in Mercy and Knowledge and forgave sins out of clemency and care. You are The Most Forgiving, Most Merciful, Clement, All-Knowing, Most Lofty and Greatest.

وَصَلَّى اللهُ عَلَى سَيِّدِنَا مُحَمَّدٍ وَعَلَى جَمِيعِ الأَنْبِيَاءِ وَالْمُرْسَلِينَ وَالحَمْدُ للهِ رَبِّ العَالَمِينْ.

wa ṣallā Allāhu ʿalā sayyidinā Muḥammadin wa ʿalā jamīʿi-l-anbiyāʾi wa-l-mursalīna wa-l-ḥamdu lillāhi Rabbil ʿĀlamīn.

May Allah send His Prayers upon our master Muhammad and all the prophets and messengers. All Praise is due to Allah the Lord of the worlds.

يَوْمِ الإِثْنَيْن

Yawmi-l-Ithnayn

The Day of Monday

اللهُمَّ إِنِّي أَسْأَلُكَ النُّورَ وَالهُدَى وَالأَدَبَ فِي الاقْتِدَاءِ، وَأَعُوذُ بِكَ مِنْ شَرِّ نَفْسِي وَمِنْ شَرِّ كُلِّ قَاطِعٍ يَقْطَعُنِي عَنْكَ لَا إِلَهَ إِلَّا أَنْتَ. اللهُمَّ قَدِّسْ نَفْسِي مِنَ الشُّبُهَاتِ وَالأَخْلَاقِ السَّيِّئَاتِ وَالحُظُوظِ وَالغَفَلَاتِ وَاجْعَلْنِي عَبْدًا مُطِيعًا لَكَ فِي جَمِيعِ الحَالَاتْ.

Allāhumma innī asʾaluka-n-nūra wa-l-hudā wa-l-adaba fi-l-iqtidāʾ, wa aʿūdhu bika min sharri nafsī wa min sharri kulli qāṭiʿin yaqṭaʿunī ʿanka lā ilāha illā Ant. Allāhumma qaddis nafsī mina-sh-shubuhāti wa-l-akhlāqi-s-sayyiʾāti wa-l-ḥuẓūẓi wa-l-ghafalāti wa-jʿalnī ʿabdan muṭīʿan laka fī jamīʿi-l-ḥālāt.

Oh Allah, I ask You for light, guidance, and proper etiquette in imitation. I seek refuge in You from the evil of my soul and from the evil of every deterrer that deters from You, there is no god but You. Oh Allah, sanctify my soul from ambiguities, lowly traits, desires, and heedlessness. Make me an obedient servant for You in all states.

يَا عَلِيمُ عَلِّمْنِي مِنْ عِلْمِك، يَا حَكِيمُ أَيِّدْنِي بِحُكْمِك، يَا سَمِيعُ أَسْمِعْنِي مِنْك، يَا بَصِيرُ بَصِّرْنِي فِي آلائِك، يَا خَبِيرُ فَهِّمْنِي عَنْك، يَا حَيُّ أَحْيِنِي بِذِكْرِك، يَا مُرِيدُ خَلِّصْ إِرَادَتِي بِمِنِّكَ وَقُدْرَتِك

وَعَظَمَتِكَ إِنَّكَ عَلَى كُلِّ شَيْءٍ قَدِيرْ.

Yā ʿAlīmu ʿallimnī min ʿilmik, yā Ḥakīmu ayyidnī bi-ḥukmik, yā Samīʿu asmiʿnī mink, yā Baṣīru baṣṣirnī fī ālāʾik, yā Khabīru fahhimnī ʿank, yā Ḥayyu aḥiynī bi-dhikrik, yā Murīdu khalliṣ irādatī bi-minnika wa qudratika wa ʿaẓamatika innaka ʿalā kulli shayʾin Qadīr.

Oh All-Knower, teach me from Your Knowledge. Oh, Most Wise, support me with Your Wisdom. Oh All-Hearing, let me hear from You. Oh All-Seeing, let me perceive Your Signs. Oh, All-Aware, let me comprehend from You. Oh All-Living, grant me life through Your Remembrance. Oh, All-Willing, purify my will with your generosity, power, and greatness. Indeed, You can do all things.

اللهُمَّ إِنِّي أَسْأَلُكَ بِاللَّاهُوتِ ذِي التَّدْبِيرِ وَالنَّاسُوتِ ذِي التَّسْخِيرِ وَالفِعْلِ ذِي التَّأْثِيرِ وَالمُحِيطُ بِالكُلِّ وَالجُمْلَةِ فِي التَّفْصِيلِ وَالتَّصْوِيرِ وَالتَّقْدِيرْ. أَسْأَلُكَ بِذَاتِكَ الَّتِي لَا تُدْرَكُ وَلَا تُتْرَكُ وَبِأَحَدِيَّتِكَ الَّتِي مَنْ تَوَهَّمَ فِيهَا المَعِيَّةَ فَقَدْ أَشْرَكَ وَإِحَاطَتِكَ الَّتِي مَنْ ظَنَّ فِي أَزَلِهَا غَيْرًا فَقَدْ أَفِكَ وَمِنْ نِظَامِ الإِخْلَاصِ فَقَدْ انْفَكَّ.

Allāhumma innī asʾaluka bi-l-lāhūti dhi-t-tadbīri wa-n-nāsūti dhi-t-taskhīri wa-l-fiʿli dhi-t-taʾthīri wa-l-muḥīṭu bi-l-kulli wa-l-jumlatī fi-t-tafṣīli wa-t-taṣwīri wa-t-taqdīr. asʾaluka bi-dhātika al-latī lā tudraku wa lā tutraku wa bi-aḥadiyyatika al-latī man tawahhama fīha-l-maʿayyata fa-qad ashraka wa iḥāṭatika al-latī man ẓanna fī azalihā

ghayran fa-qad afika wa min niẓāmi-l-ikhlāṣi fa-qad infakk.
Oh Allah, I ask You by the Divinity that manages affairs, Humanity in submission and Your Acts of affection that encompass all entirely, in detail, form and measure. I ask You through Your Essence that can neither be comprehended nor left, and through Your Singularity, with which anyone assumes partnership, then they have committed polytheism, and through Your Envelopment, about whose eternality anyone assumes otherwise, then they have sinned and deviated from the law of sincerity.

يَا مَنْ سُلِبَ عَنْهُ تَنْزِيهًا مَا لَمْ يَكُنْ فِي قِدَمِهِ يَا مَنْ قَدِرَ عَلَى كُلِّ شَيْءٍ بِإِحَاطَتِهِ وَعَظَمَتِهِ يَا مَنْ أَبْرَزَ نُورَ كُلِّ وُجُودِهِ مِنْ ظُلْمَةِ عَدَمِهِ يَا مَنْ صَوَّرَ أَشْخَاصَ الأَفْلَاكِ بِمَا أَوْدَعَ مِنْ عِلْمِهِ فِي قَلَمِهِ يَا مَنْ صَرَّفَ أَحْكَامَهُ بِأَسْرَارِ حِكَمِهِ أُنَادِيكَ اسْتِغَاثَةَ بَعِيدٍ لِقَرِيبٍ وَأَطْلُبُكَ طَلَبَ مُحِبٍّ لِحَبِيبْ

Yā man suliba ʿanhu tanzīhan mā lam yakun fī qidamihi yā man qadira ʿalā kulli shayʾin bi-iḥāṭatihi wa ʿaẓamatihi yā man abraza nūra kulla wujūdihi min ẓulmati ʿadamihi yā man ṣawwara ashkhāṣa-l-aflāki bi-mā awdaʿa min ʿilmihi fī qalamihi yā man ṣarrafa aḥkāmahu bi-asrāri ḥikamihi unādīka istighāthata baʿīdin li-Qarībin wa aṭlubuka ṭalaba muḥibbin li-Ḥabīb

Oh, You from whom has been negated every transcendence that does not befit His Eternality. Oh You, who has overcome everything with His

Envelopment and Greatness. Oh, You who brings out the light of all His Being [creation] from within the darkness of its non-existence. Oh You, who molded the persons of orbits with what He has bestowed of His Knowledge in His Pen. Oh You, who has delegated the secrets of His Wisdoms to His Rulings. I call upon You with the implore of one who is far, seeking He who is Near, and I seek You with the seeking of a lover for their Beloved.

وَأَسْأَلُكَ سُؤَالَ مُضْطَرٍّ لِمُجِيبْ. أَسْأَلُكَ اللهُمَّ رَفْعَ حِجَابَ الغَيْبِ وَحَلَّ عِقَالَ الرَّيْبْ. اللهُمَّ أَحْيِنِي بِحَيَاتِكَ حَيَاةً وَاجِبَةً وَعَلِّمْنِي كَذَلِكَ عِلْمًا مُحِيطًا بِأَسْرَارِ المَعْلُومَاتِ وَافْتَحْ لِي بِقُدْرَتِكَ كَنْزَ الجَنَّةِ وَالعَرْشِ وَالذَّاتِ وَامْحَقْنِي تَحْتَ أَنْوَارِ الصِّفَاتِ وَخَلِّصْنِي بِمَنِّكَ مِنْ جَمِيعِ القُيُودِ المُقَيِّدَاتْ

wa as'aluka su'āla muḍṭarrin li-Mujīb. as'aluka Allāhumma raf'a ḥijāba-l-ghaybi wa ḥalla 'iqāla-r-rayb. Allāhumma aḥiynī bi-ḥayātika ḥayātan wājibatan wa 'allimnī ka-dhālika 'ilman muḥīṭan bi-asrāri-l-ma'lūmāti wa-ftaḥ lī bi-qudratika kanza-l-jannati wa-l-'arshi wa-dh-dhāti wa-mḥaqnī taḥta anwāri-ṣ-ṣifāti wa khalliṣnī bi-mannika min jamī'i-l-quyūdi-l-muqayyidāt

I ask You with the implore of one who is need towards One who Responds. I ask You, oh Allah, for the lifting of the veil of the unseen and untying the knot of doubt. Oh Allah, enliven me with Your Life, that obligatory life, and teach me a knowledge that encompasses the secrets of known things. Open for me, with Your Power, the treasuries of paradise, throne, and Essence. Efface me under the lights of Divine Attributes and purify me, through Your Gifts, from all imprisoning chains

سُبْحَانَكَ تَنْزِيهًا سُبُّوحٌ تَنَزَّهَ عَنْ سِمَاتِ الْحُدُوثِ وَصِفَاتِ النَّقْصْ. قُدُّوسٌ تَطَهَّرَ مِنْ أَشْيَاءِ الذَّمِّ وَمُوجِبَاتِ الرَّفْضْ. سُبْحَانَكَ أَعْجَزْتَ كُلَّ طَالِبٍ عَنِ الْوُصُولِ إِلَيْكَ إِلَّا بِكْ. سُبْحَانَكَ لَا يَعْلَمُ مَنْ أَنْتَ سِوَاكْ. سُبْحَانَكَ مَا أَقْرَبُكَ مَعَ تَرَفُّعِ عُلَاكْ.

Subḥānaka tanzīhan Subbūḥun tanazzaha ʿan simāti-l-ḥudūthi wa ṣifāti-n-naqṣ. Quddūsun taṭahhara min ashyāʾi-dh-dhammi wa mūjibāti-r-rafḍ. Subḥānaka aʿjazta kulla ṭālibin ʿani-l-wuṣūli ilayka illā bik. Subḥānaka lā yaʿlamu man Anta siwāk. Subḥānaka mā aqrabuka maʿa taraffuʿi ʿulāk.

Glory be to You in transcendence. Most-Glorified One who is Sanctified from the traits of accidents and attributes of deformity. Most-Sanctified who is Purified from the blameworthy things and obligations of denial. Glory be to You; You have dumbfounded every seeker from reaching You save through You. Glory be to You, no one knows You save You. Glory be to You, how Near You are in Your Elevated Exaltedness.

اللهُمَّ أَلْبِسْنِي سُبْحَةَ الحَمْدِ وَرَدِّنِي بِرِدَاءِ العِزِّ وَتَوِّجْنِي بِتَاجِ الجَلَالِ وَالمَجْدِ وَجَرِّدْنِي عَنْ صِفَاتِ الهَزَلِ وَالجِدِّ. وَخَلِّصْنِي مِنْ قُيُودِ العَدَدِ وَالحَدِّ وَمُبَاشَرَةِ الخِلَافِ وَالنَقِيضِ وَالضِّدِّ. إِلَهِي عَدَمِي بِكَ عَيْنُ الوُجودِ، وَبَقَائِي مَعَكَ عَيْنُ العَدَمْ.

Allāhumma albisnī subḥata-l-ḥamdi wa raddinī bi-ridāʾi-l-ʿizzi wa tawwijnī bi-tāji-l-jalāli wa-l-majdi wa jarridnī ʿan ṣifāti-l-hazli wa-l-jidd. wa khalliṣnī min quyūdi-l-ʿadadi wa-l-ḥaddi wa mubāsharati-l-khilāfi wa-n-naqīḍi wa-ḍ-ḍidd. Ilāhī ʿadamī bika ʿaynu-l-wujūdi wa baqāʾī maʿaka ʿaynu-l-ʿadam.

Oh Allah, dress me with the garment of praise, clothe me with the dress of exaltedness, crown me with the crown of majesty and honor and dissolve me of both, the attributes of mockery and seriousness. Purify me from the chains of number and boundaries and direction towards conflict, contradiction, and opposition. Oh Allah, my non-existence through You is the essence of existence. While my subsistence with You is the essence of non-existence.

فَأَبْدِلْنِي مَكَانَ تَوَهُّمِ وُجودِي مَعَكَ بِتَحْقِيقِ عَدَمِي بِكَ، وَاجْمَعْ شَمْلِي بِاسْتِهْلَاكِي فِيكْ. لَا إِلَهَ إِلَّا أَنْتَ تَنَزَّهْتَ عَنْ المَثِيلْ. لَا إِلَهَ إِلَّا أَنْتَ تَعَالَيْتَ عَنْ النَّظِيرْ. لَا إِلَهَ إِلَّا أَنْتَ اسْتَغْنَيْتَ عَنْ الوَزِيرِ وَالمُشِيرْ. لَا إِلَهَ إِلَّا أَنْتَ يَا مُغِيثُ يَا أَحَدُ يَا صَمَدْ.

fa-abdilnī makāna tawahhumi wujūdī maʿaka bi-taḥqīqi ʿadamī bika wa-jmaʿ shamlī bi-stihlākī fik. lā ilāha illā Anta tanazzahta ʿani-l-mathīl. lā ilāha illā Anta taʿālayta ʿani-n-naẓīr. lā ilāha illā Anta-staghnayta ʿani-l-wazīri wa-l-mushīr. lā ilāha illā Anta yā Mughīthu yā Aḥadu yā Ṣamad.

So, exchange for me, in place of my illusive existence with You the realization of my non-existence through You. Gather my unity through being consumed in You. There is no god but You, You are Sanctified from having a similar. There is no god but You, You are Elevated from having an equal. There is no god but You, You are Sufficed from needing a minister and helper. There is no god but You, oh Savior, Singular and Self-Sufficient.

لَا إِلَهَ إِلَّا أَنْتَ بِكَ الوُجُودُ وَلَكَ السُجودُ وَأَنْتَ الحَقُّ المَعْبُودْ أَعُوذُ بِكَ مِنِّي وَأَسْأَلُكَ زَوَالِي عَنِّي وَأَسْتَغْفِرُكَ مَنْ بَقِيَّةِ تَبعُّدٍ وَتَدَنِّي وَتَسَمِّي وَتَكَنِّي. أَنْتَ الوَاضِعُ وَالرَّافِعُ وَالْمُبْدِعُ وَالقَاطِعُ وَالْمُفَرِّقُ وَالجَامِعْ. يَا وَاضِعُ يَا رَافِعُ يَا مُبْدِعُ يَا قَاطِعُ يَا مُفَرِّقُ يَا جَامِعْ.

lā ilāha illā Anta bika-l-wujūdu wa laka-s-sujūdu wa anta-l-Ḥaqqu-l-Maʿbūd. aʿūdhu bika minni wa asʾaluka zawālī ʿannī wa astaghfiruka min baqiyyati tabaʿʿudin wa tadannī wa tasammī wa takannī. Anta-l-Wāḍiʿu wa-r-Rāfiʿu wa-l-Mubdiʿu wa-l-Qāṭiʿu wa-l-Mufarriqu wa-l-Jāmiʿ. yā Wāḍiʿu yā Rāfiʿu ya Mubdiʿu yā Qāṭiʿu yā Mufarriqu yā Jāmiʿ.

There is no god but You, through You is existence, to

You is prostration and You are the Real Worshipped One. I seek refuge in You from me, ask You my annihilation from myself, and seek Your Forgiveness from any remainder of distance, lowliness, stigma, and labels. You are the Abaser, Elevator, Beginner, Cutter, Disperser and Gatherer. Oh Abaser, Elevator, Beginner, Cutter, Disperser and Gatherer.

العِيَاذُ العِيَاذُ الغِيَاثُ الغِيَاثْ. النَّجَاةُ النَّجَاةُ المَلَاذُ المَلَاذْ. يَا مَنْ بِهِ نَجَاتِي وَمَلَاذِي. أَسْأَلُكَ فِيمَا سَأَلْتُكَ وَأَتَوَسَّلُ إِلَيْكَ بِمُقَدِّمَةِ الوُجودِ الأَوَّلِ وَنُورِ العِلْمِ الأَكْمَلِ وَرُوحِ الحَيَاةِ الأَفْضَلِ وَبِسَاطِ الرَّحْمَةِ الأَزَلِ وَسَمَاءِ الخُلُقِ الأَجَلِّ، وَالسَّابِقِ بِالرُّوحِ وَالفَضْلِ وَالخَاتَمِ بِالصُّوَرِ وَالبَعْثْ.

al-ʿiyādhu-l-ʿiyādhu-l-ghiyāthu-l-ghiyāth. An-najātu-n-najātu-l-malādhu-l-malādh. yā man bihi najātī wa malādhī. asʾaluka fī-mā saʾaltuka wa atawassalu ilayka bi-muqaddimati-l-wujūdi-l-awwali wa nūri-l-ʿilmi-l-akmali wa rūḥi-l-ḥayāti-l-afḍali wa bisāṭi-r-raḥmati-l-azali wa samāʾi-l-khuluqi-l-ajalli wa-s-sābiqi bi-r-rūḥi wa-l-faḍli wa-l-khātami bi-ṣ-ṣuwari wa-l-baʿth.

Grant refuge! Grant relief! Grant salvation! Grant protection! Oh, You through whom is my salvation and protection. I ask You through everything I have asked and seek the intercession of the beginning of the first existent, light of the perfect knowledge, spirit of the best life, platform of the pre-eternal mercy, heaven of the noblest character, the one preceding in spirit and honor and he who seals forms and resurrection.

وَالنُّورِ بِالهِدَايَةِ وَالبَيَانِ وَالرَّحْمَةِ بِالعِلْمِ وَالتَّمْكِينِ وَالإِيمَانْ. مُحَمَّدٍ الْمُصْطَفَى وَالرَّسُولِ الْمُجْتَبَى صَلَّى اللهُ تَعَالَى عَلَيْهِ وَعَلَى آلِهِ وَصَحْبِهِ وَسَلَّمَ تَسْلِيمًا كَثِيرًا إِلَى يَوْمِ الدِّينِ وَالحَمْدُ للهِ رَبِّ العَالَمِينْ.

wa-n-nūri bi-l-hidāyati wa-l-bayāni wa-r-raḥmati bi-l-ʿilmi wa-t-tamkīni wa-l-īmān. Muḥammadini-l-muṣṭafā wa-r-rasūli-l-mujtabā ṣallā Allāhu taʿālā ʿalayhi wa ʿalā ālihi wa ṣaḥbihi wa sallama taslīman kathīran ilā yawmi-d-dīni wa-l-ḥamdu lillāhi Rabbi-l-ʿālamīn.

The light of guidance and clarity, mercy of knowledge, consolidation, and faith. Muhammad ﷺ the chosen, the designated messenger. May Allah the Exalted send prayers upon him, his family, and companions with abundant salutations until the Day of Judgment. All praise is due to Allah the Lord of the worlds.

لَيْلَةُ الثُّلَاثَاءِ

Laylatu-th-Thulāthā'

The Night of Tuesday

إِلَهِي أَنْتَ شَدِيدُ الْبَطْشِ أَلِيمُ الْأَخْذِ عَظِيمُ الْقَهْرِ الْمُتَعَالِي عَنِ الْأَضْدَادِ وَالْأَنْدَادِ وَالْمُنَزَّهِ عَنِ الصَّاحِبَةِ وَالْأَوْلَادِ. شَأْنُكَ قَهْرُ الْأَعْدَاءِ وَقَمْعُ الْجَبَّارِينَ، تَمْكُرُ بِمَنْ تَشَاءُ وَأَنْتَ خَيْرُ الْمَاكِرِينْ

Ilāhī Anta Shadīdu-l-Baṭshi Alīmu-l-Akhdhi ʿAẓīmu-l-Qahri-l-Mutaʿālī ʿani-l-aḍdādi wa-l-andādi wa-l-Munazzahi ʿani-ṣ-ṣāḥibati wa-l-awlād. shaʾnuka qahru-l-aʿdāʾi wa qamʿu-l-jabbārīna tamkuru bi-man tashāʾu wa Anta khayru-l-mākirīn

Oh Allah, You are Swift in Assault, Severe in Chastisement, Great in Subduing, Exalted of oppositions and competitors and Sanctified from having a spouse and children. Your Affair is to subdue enemies and destroy tyrants. Your Cunning is with whom You Will. Indeed, You are the best of planners

أَسْأَلُكَ بِإِسْمِكَ الَّذِي أَخَذْتَ بِهِ النَّوَاصِي وَأَنْزَلْتَ بِهِ مِنَ الصَّيَاصِي وَقَذَفْتَ بِهِ الرُّعْبَ فِي قُلُوبِ الْأَعْدَاءِ وَأَشْقَيْتَ بِهِ أَهْلَ الشَّقَاءِ أَنْ تُمِدَّنِي بِرَقِيقَةٍ مِنْ رَقَائِقِ إِسْمِكَ الشَّرِيفِ تَسْرِي فِي قُوَايَ الْقَلْبِيَّةِ وَالْقَالِبِيَّةِ حَتَّى أَتَمَكَّنَ مِنْ فِعْلِ مَا أُرِيدْ

as'aluka bi-ismika al-ladhī akhadhta bihi-n-nawāṣī wa anzalta bihi mina-ṣ-ṣayāṣī wa qadhafta bihi-r-ruʿba fī qulūbi-l-aʿdāʾi wa ashqayta bihi ahla-sh-shaqāʾi an tumiddanī bi-raqīqatin min raqāʾiqi ismika-sh-Sharīfi tasrī fī quwāya-l-qalbiyyati wa-l-qālibiyyati ḥattā atamakkana min fiʿli mā urīd

I ask You by Your Name through which You taken foreheads, coaxed [enemies] out of fortresses, cast fear in the hearts of enemies and made miserable through it the people of misery, that You sustain me with a subtlety from the subtleties of Your Name The Noble[42] to permeate my faculties, in heart and form, so that I can do what I will

فَلَا يَصِلُ إِلَيَّ ظَالِمٌ بِظُلْمٍ وَلَا يَسْطُو عَلَيَّ مُتَكَبِّرٍ بِجَوْرْ. وَاجْعَلْ غَضَبِي لَكَ وَفِيكَ مَقْرُونًا بِغَضَبِكَ لِنَفْسِكْ. وَاطْمِسْ عَلَى وُجُوهِ أَعْدَائِي وَاشْدُدْ عَلَى قُلُوبِهِمْ وَامْسَخْهُمْ عَلَى مَكَانَتِهِمْ وَاضْرِبْ بَيْنِي وَبَيْنَهُمْ ﴿بِسُورٍ لَهُ بَابٌ بَاطِنُهُ فِيهِ الرَّحْمَةُ وَظَاهِرُهُ مِنْ قِبَلِهِ الْعَذَابْ﴾[43]

fa-lā yaṣilu ilayya ẓālimun bi-ẓulmin wa lā yasṭū ʿalayya mutakabbirin bi-jawr. wa-jʿal ghaḍabī laka wa fīka maqrūnan bi-ghaḍabika li-nafsik. wa-ṭmis ʿalā wujūhi aʿdāʾī wa-shdud ʿalā qulūbihim wa-msakhhum ʿalā makānatihim wa-ḍrib baynī wa baynahum "Bi-sūrin lahu bābun bāṭinuhu fīhi-r-raḥmatu wa ẓāhiruhu min qibalihi-l-ʿadhāb"

---

[42] Alternatively, this can also be read 'from Your Noble Name'

[43] الحديد 13

So that no unjust person can reach me with their injustice, nor a transgressor with their oppression. Make my anger for and within you connected with Your Anger for Yourself. Efface the faces of my enemies, constrict their hearts, deform them in their places, and erect between me and them "A barrier that has a door, its inward is mercy while its outward manifests as punishment."

إِنَّكَ شَدِيدُ البَطْشِ أَلِيمُ الأَخْذِ وَالعِقَابْ، ﴿وَكَذَٰلِكَ أَخْذُ رَبِّكَ إِذَا أَخَذَ القُرَىٰ وَهِيَ ظَٰلِمَةٌ إِنَّ أَخْذَهُۥٓ أَلِيمٌ شَدِيدٌ﴾[44] رَبِّ أَغْنِنِي بِكَ عَمَّنْ سِوَاكَ غِنًى يُغْنِنِي غَايَةَ الغِنَا عَنْ كُلِّ حَظٍّ يَدْعُونِي إِلَى ظَاهِرِ خَلْقٍ أَوْ بَاطِنِ أَمْرٍ

innaka Shadīdu-l-Baṭshi Alīmu-l-Akhdhi wa-l-ʿiqāb, "Wa ka-dhālika akhdhu Rabbika idhā akhadha-l-qurā wa hiya ẓālimatun inna akhdhahu alīmun shadīd" Rabbi aghninī bika ʿamman siwāka ghinan yughninī ghāyata-l-ghinā ʿan kulli ḥaẓẓin yadʿūnī ilā ẓāhiri khalqin aw bāṭini amrin

Indeed, You are Swift in Assault, Severe in Chastisement, and punishment, "Like so is the chastisement of your Lord when He takes the towns as they transgress. Indeed, His Chastisement is painful and severe" My Lord, suffice me through You from other than You, a sufficiency that enriches me absolutely from every share that calls me to the outward of a created being

---

[44] هود 102

or the inward of a command.

وَبَلِّغْنِي غَايَةَ تَيْسِيرِي وَارْفَعْنِي إِلَى سِدْرَةِ مُنْتَهَايَ وَاشْهِدْنِي الوُجودَ كَرَوِيًّا وَالسَّيْرَ دَوْرِيًّا لِأُعَايِنَ سِرَّ التَّنَزُّلِ إِلَى النِّهَايَاتِ وَالعَوْدِ إِلَى البِدَايَاتِ حَتَّى يَنْقَطِعُ الكَلَامُ وَتَسْكُنُ حَرَكَةُ الأَقْلَامِ وَتُمْحَى نُقْطَةُ الغَيْنِ وَيَعُودُ الوَاحِدُ إِلَى الإِثْنَيْنْ

wa ballighnī ghāyata taysīrī wa-rfaʿnī ilā sidrati muntahāya wa-ashhidnī-l-wujūda karawiyyan wa-s-sayra dawriyyan li-uʿāyina sirra-t-tanazzuli ila-n-nihāyāti wa-l-ʿawdi ila-l-bidāyāti ḥattā yanqaṭiʿu-l-kalāmu wa taskunu ḥarakatu-l-aqlāmi wa tumḥā nuqṭatu-l-ghayni wa yaʿūdu-l-wāḥidu ila-l-ithnayn

Deliver me to my utmost felicity, raise me to my Lote Tree and grant me to witness existence circularly and traveling cyclically, so that I may perceive the secret of descent to the ends and return to the beginnings, until speech halts, the movement of pens comes to a still, the dot of density disappears[45] and the One returns to two

إِلَهِي يَسِّرْ عَلَيَّ بِالسِّرِّ الَّذِي تَسَتَّرَ عَلَى كَثِيرٍ مِنْ الخَلْقِ وَيَسَّرْتَهُ عَلَى كَثِيرٍ مِنْ أَوْلِيَائِكَ تَيْسِيرًا يُعْجِمُ عَيْنَ عَنَائِي وَيَكْشِفُ عَنِّي نُورَ

---

45 The Shaykh here is masterfully using the two Arabic letters *ghayn* and *ʿayn*, that are calligraphically related (غ ، ع) and mean density and essence, respectively. Thus, when the dot of the density (i.e., letter ghayn) is removed, one is left with the letter ʿayn (i.e., the Divine Essence appears).

أَعْدَائِي وَأَيِّدْ لِي ذَلِكَ بِنُورٍ شَعْشَعَانِيٍّ يَخْطِفُ بَصَرَ كُلِّ حَاسِدٍ مِنَ الْجِنِّ وَالْإِنْسِ

Ilāhī yassir ʿalayya bi-s-sirri-l-ladhī tasattara ʿalā kathīrin mina-l-khalqi wa yassartahu ʿalā kathīrin min awliyāʾika taysīran yuʿjimu ʿayna ʿanāʾī wa yakshifu ʿannī nūra aʿdāʾī wa ayyid lī dhālika bi-nūrin shaʿshaʿāniyyin yakhṭifu baṣara kulli ḥāsidin mina-l-jinni wa-l-ins

Oh Allah, facilitate for me, through the secret that has been curtailed from many created beings, yet facilitated for many of Your Saints, to make my tiredness speechless, unveils for me the light of my enemies and aid me in this with a radiating light that captivates the sights of every envious human and demon

وَهَبْ لِي مَلَكَةَ الْغَلَبَةِ بِكُلِّ مَقَامٍ وَاَغْنِنِي بِكَ غِنًى يُثْبِتُ فَقْرِي إِلَيْكَ إِنَّكَ أَنْتَ الْغَنِيُّ الْمَجِيدُ وَالْوَلِيُّ الْحَمِيدُ الْكَرِيمُ الرَّشِيدْ. وَصَلَّى اللهُ عَلَى سَيِّدِنَا مُحَمَّدٍ وَعَلَى آلِهِ وَصَحْبِهِ أَجْمَعِينَ وَالْحَمْدُ للهِ رَبِّ الْعَالَمِينْ.

wa hab lī malakata-l-ghalabati bi-kulli maqāmin wa aghninī bika ghinan yuthbitu faqrī ilayka innaka Anta-l-Ghaniyyu-l-Majīdu wa-l-Waliyyu-l-Ḥamīdu-l-Karīmu-r-Rashīd. wa ṣallā Allāhu ʿalā sayyidina Muḥammadin wa ʿalā ālihi wa ṣaḥbihi ajmaʿīna wa-l-ḥamdu lillāhi Rabbil ʿālamīn.

Grant me an aura of victory in every station. Suffice me through You, to establish my need for You. You are the Self-Sufficient, Most Honorable, Guardian,

Most Praiseworthy, Most Generous and Guide. May Allah send His Prayers upon our master Muhammad, his family, and companions entirely. All Praise is due to Allah the Lord of the worlds.

يَوْمُ الثُّلَاثَاء

Yawmu-th-Thulāthā'

The Day of Tuesday

رَبِّ أَدْخِلْنِي فِي لُجَّةِ بَحْرِ أَحَدِيَّتِكَ وَطَمْطَامِ يَمِّ وَاحِدِيَّتِكَ وَقَوِّنِي بِسَطْوَةِ سُلْطَانِ فَرْدَانِيَّتِكَ حَتَّى أَخْرُجَ إِلَى سَعَةِ فَضَاءِ رَحْمَتِكْ، وَفِي وَجْهِي لَمَعَانُ بَرْقِ الْقُرْبِ مِنْ آثَارِ رَحْمَتِكْ، مَهِيبًا بِهَيْبَتِكَ عَزِيزًا بِعِزَّتِكَ مَعِينًا بِعِنَايَتِكَ مُبَجَّلًا مُكَرَّمًا بِتَعْلِيمِكَ وَتَرْبِيَتِكْ.

Rabbi adkhilnī fī lujjati baḥri aḥadiyyatika wa ṭamṭāmi yammi wāḥidiyyatika wa qawwinī bi-saṭwati sulṭāni fardāniyyatika ḥattā akhruja ilā sa'ati faḍā'i raḥmatik, wa fī wajhī lama'ānu barqi-l-qurbi min āthāri raḥmatik mahīban bi-haybatika 'azīzan bi-'izzatika ma'īnan bi-'ināyatika mubajjalan mukarraman bi-ta'līmika wa tarbiyatik.

Oh, my Lord, admit me into the depth of the ocean of Your Singularity and the cascading shore of Your Oneness. Strengthen me with the reach of the authority of Your Uniqueness, so that I may exit to the expansiveness of the space of Your Mercy, with the luminous flash of nearness from the traces of Your Mercy on my face, made awe-inspiring by Your Awe, exalted by Your Exaltation, aided by Your Attentiveness, ennobled, and honored by Your Teaching and Discipline.

اللهُمَّ أَلْبِسْنِي خِلَعَ الْعِزَّةِ وَالْقَبُولْ، وَانْهَجْ لِي مَنَاهِجَ الْوَصْلَةِ وَالْوُصُولْ، وَتَوِّجْنِي بِتَاجِ الْكَرَامَةِ وَالْوَقَارْ، وَأَلِّفْ بَيْنِي وَبَيْنَ

أَحِبَّائِكَ فِي دَارِ الدُّنْيَا وَدَارِ الْقَرَارِ، وَارْزُقْنِي مِنْ نُورِ أَسْمَائِكَ بِنُورِ اسْمِكَ هَيْبَةً وَسَطْوَةً حَتَّى تَنْقَادَ إِلَيَّ الْقُلُوبُ وَالْأَرْوَاحُ وَتَخْضَعَ لَدَيَّ النُّفُوسُ وَالْأَشْبَاحُ.

Allāhumma albisnī khilaʿa-l-ʿizzati wa-l-qabūl, wa-nhaj lī manāhija-l-waṣlati wa-l-wuṣūl, wa tawwijnī bi-tāji-l-karāmati wa-l-waqār, wa allif baynī wa bayna aḥibbāʾika fī dāri-d-dunyā wa dāri-l-qarār, wa-rzuqnī min nūri asmāʾika bi-nūri ismika haybatan wa saṭwatan ḥattā tanqāda ilayya-l-qulūbu wa-l-arwāḥu wa takhḍaʿa ladayya-n-nufūsu wa-l-ashbāḥ.

Oh Allah, clothe me with the garments of exaltation and acceptance, set out for me the ways of intimacy and arrival, crown me with the crown of honor and regality, harmonize between me and Your Loved Ones in this world and the hereafter. Sustain me from the Light of Your Names, through the Light of Your Name[46], such that hearts and spirits follow me, and souls and apparitions submit to me.

يَا مَنْ ذَلَّتْ لَهُ رِقَابُ الْجَبَابِرَةِ وَخَضَعَتْ لَهُ أَعْنَاقُ الْأَكَاسِرَةْ، لَا مَلْجَأَ وَلَا مَنْجَا مِنْكَ وَلَا إِعَانَةَ إِلَّا بِكَ وَلَا اتِّكَالَ إِلَّا عَلَيْكَ. ادْفَعْ عَنِّي كَيْدَ الْحَاسِدِينَ وَظُلُمَاتِ شَرِّ الْمُعَانِدِينَ وَاحْفَظْنِي وَارْحَمْنِي وَاجْعَلْنِي تَحْتَ سُرَادِقَاتِ عِزَّتِكَ يَا أَرْحَمَ الرَّاحِمِينْ.

---

[46] The distinction between Name and Names here is between the Allah's Greatest Name and His other Names.

yā man dhallat lahu riqābu-l-jababirati wa khaḍaʿat lahu aʿnāqu-l-akāsirah, lā maljaʾa wa lā manjā minka wa lā iʿānata illā bika wa la-t-tikāla illā ʿalayk. idfaʿ ʿannī kayda-l-ḥāsidīna wa ẓulumāti sharri-l-muʿānidīna wa-ḥfaẓnī wa-rḥamnī wa-jʿalnī taḥta surādiqāti ʿizzatika yā Arḥama-r-Rāḥimīn.

Oh You, to whom were humbled the necks of tyrants and submitted the heads of caesars, there is neither haven nor salvation from You, no aid except through You and no dependence save upon You. Keep away from me the connivance of the envious and darknesses of the evil of the stubborn. Protect and have mercy upon me and make me under the treasuries of Your Exaltation oh Most Merciful of the merciful.

إِلَهِي أَيِّدْ ظَاهِرِي وَبَاطِنِي فِي تَحْصِيلِ مَرَاضِيكْ، وَنَوِّرْ قَلْبِي وَسِرِّي لِلإِطِّلَاعِ عَلَى مَنَاهِجِ مَسَاعِيكْ. إِلَهِي كَيْفَ أُصَدُّ عَنْ بَابِكَ بِخَيْبَةٍ مِنْكَ وَقَدْ وَرَدْتُهُ عَلَى ثِقَةٍ مِنْكْ وَكَيْفَ تُؤَيِّسُنِي مِنْ عَطَائِكَ وَقَدْ أَمَرْتَنِي بِدُعَائِكْ. وَهَا أَنَا مُقْبِلٌ عَلَيْكَ مُلْتَجِئٌ إِلَيْكْ.

Ilāhī ayyid ẓāhirī wa bāṭinī fi taḥṣīli marāḍīk, wa nawwir qalbī wa sirrī li-l-iṭṭilāʿi ʿalā manāhiji masāʿīk. Ilāhī kayfa uṣaddu ʿan bābika bi-khaybatin minka wa qad waradtuhu ʿalā thiqatin mink wa kayfa tuʾayyisunī min ʿaṭāʾika wa qad amartanī bi-duʿāʾik. wa hā anā muqbilun ʿalayka multajiʾun ilayk.

Oh Allah, support my outward and inward in gaining Your Contentment. Illuminate my heart and secret to discover the ways to You. Oh Allah, how can I be turned away from Your Door with disappointment when I arrived at it with confidence in You? How would You deprive me of the hope to receive Your Bounties when You commanded me to supplicate to You? Here I am, coming towards You and seeking Your Refuge.

بَاعِدْ بَيْنِي وَبَيْنَ أَعْدَائِي كَمَا بَاعَدْتَ بَيْنَ الْمَشْرِقِ وَالْمَغْرِبْ، وَاخْطَفْ أَبْصَارَهُمْ وَزَلْزِلْ أَقْدَامَهُمْ وَادْفَعْ عَنِّي شَرَّهُمْ وَضُرَّهُمْ بِنُورِ قُدْسِكَ وَجَلَالِ مَجْدِكَ إِنَّكَ أَنْتَ اللهُ مُعْطِي جَلَائِلَ النِّعَمْ، الْمُبَجِّلُ الْمُكَرِمُ لِمَنْ نَاجَاكَ بِلَطَائِفِ الرَّأْفَةِ وَالرَّحْمَةْ.

bāʿid baynī wa bayna aʿdāʾī ka-mā bāʿadta bayna-l-mashriqi wa-l-maghrib, wa-khṭaf abṣārahum wa zalzil aqdāmahum wa-dfaʿ ʿannī sharrahum wa ḍurrahum bi-nūri qudsika wa jalāli majdika innaka Anta Allāhu muʿṭī jalāʾila-n-niʿam, al-Mubajjilu-l-Mukrimu li-man najāka bi-laṭāʾifi-r-raʾfati wa-r-raḥmah.

Distance between me and my enemies as You have distanced between the east and west. Take their sights, shake their footings, and keep away from me their evil and harm through the Light of Your Sanctity and Majesty of Your Nobility. Indeed, You are Allah, the Giver of Distinguished Bounties, the One who Honors and Appreciates he who calls upon You, with subtleties of kindness and mercy.

وَاحْفَظْنِي بِجَلَالِ قُدْسِكَ وَمَجْدِكَ إِنَّكَ أَنْتَ اللهُ لَا إِلَهَ إِلَّا أَنْتَ وَحْدَكَ لَا شَرِيكَ لَكَ وَنَشْهَدُ أَنَّ سَيِّدِنَا مُحَمَّدًا عَبْدُكَ وَرَسُولُكَ وَحَبِيبُكَ وَصَفِيُّكْ. يَا حَيُّ يَا قَيُّومُ يَا كَاشِفَ الأَسْرَارِ وَالمَعَارِفِ وَالعُلُومْ.

wa-ḥfaẓnī bi-jalāli qudsika wa majdika innaka Anta Allāhu lā ilāha illā Anta waḥdaka lā sharīka laka wa nashhadu anna sayyidinā Muḥammadan ʿabduka wa rasūluka wa ḥabībuka wa ṣafiyyuk. yā Ḥayyu yā Qayyūmu yā Kāshifa-l-asrāri wa-l-maʿārifi wa-l-ʿulūm.

Preserve me through the majesty of Your Sanctity and Nobility. Indeed, You are Allah, there is no god but only You. You have no partners. We also bare witness that our master Muhammad ﷺ is Your Servant, Messenger, Beloved and Chosen One. Oh, Eternally Living and Self-Standing. Oh, Revealer of secrets, gnoses and knowledges.

وَصَلَّى اللهُ عَلَى رُوحِ سَيِّدِنَا مُحَمَّدٍ فِي الأَرْوَاحْ، وَعَلَى جَسَدِهِ فِي الأَجْسَادِ وَعَلَى قَبْرِهِ فِي القُبُورِ وَعَلَى آلِهِ وَصَحْبِهِ أَجْمَعِينْ. سُبْحَانَ رَبِّكَ رَبِّ العِزَّةِ عَمَّا يَصِفُونَ وَسَلَامٌ عَلَى المُرْسَلِينَ وَالحَمْدُ للهِ رَبِّ العَالَمِينْ.

wa ṣallā Allāhu ʿalā rūḥi sayyidinā Muḥammadin fi-l-arwāḥ, wa ʿalā jasadihi fi-l-ajsādi wa ʿalā qabrihi fi-l-qubūri wa ʿalā ālihi wa ṣaḥbihi ajmaʿīn. Subḥāna Rabbika Rabbi-l-ʿIzzati ʿammā yaṣifūna wa salāmun ʿala-l-mursalīna wa-l-

ḥamdu lillāhi Rabbil ʿālamīn.

And may Allah send His Prayers upon the spirit of our master Muhammad ﷺ among the spirits, his body among the bodies, his grave among the graves and upon his entire family and companions. Glorified be your Lord, the Lord of Exaltation, of what they describe, salutations upon the messengers and all praise is due to Allah the Lord of the worlds.

لَيْلَةُ الأَرْبُعَاء

Laylatu-l-Arbuʿāʾ

The Night of Wednesday

إِلَهِي اسْمُكَ سَيِّدُ الأَسْمَاءِ وَبِيَدِكَ مَلَكُوتِ الأَرْضِ وَالسَّمَاءْ، وَأَنْتَ القَائِمُ بِكُلِّ شَيْء. ثَبُتَ لَكَ الغِنَا وَافْتَقَرَ إِلَى فَيْضِ جُودِكَ الأَقْدَسِ كُلُّ مَا سِوَاكْ. أَسْأَلُكَ بِاسْمِكَ الَّذِي جَمَعْتَ بِهِ بَيْنَ المُتَقَابِلَاتِ وَمُتَفَرِّقَاتِ الخَلْقِ وَالأَمْرِ وَأَقَمْتَ بِهِ غَيْبَ كُلِّ ظَاهِرٍ وَأَظْهَرْتَ بِهِ كُلَّ غَائِبٍ

Ilāhī ismuka sayyidu-l-asmāʾi wa bi-yadika malakuti-l-arḍi wa-s-samāʾ, wa anta-l-Qāʾimu bi-kulli shayʾ. thabata laka-l-ghinā wa-ftaqra ilā fayḍi jūdika-l-aqdasi kullu mā siwāk. asʾaluka bi-Ismika al-ladhī jamaʿta bihi bayna-l-mutaqābilāti wa mutafarriqāti-l-khalqi wa-l-amri wa aqamta bihi ghayba kulli ẓāhirin wa aẓharta bihi kulla ghāʾib.

Oh Allah, Your Name is the Master of names, and in Your Hands is the dominion of earth and heaven. You are the sufficer of everything. Sufficiency is established for You and all other than You is impoverished, in need of the Flood of Your Holiest Munificence. I ask You by Your Name through which You have brought together oppositions and the dispersions of creation and command, and through which You have established the unseen of every outward and manifested every unseen

أَنْ تَهَبَ لِي صَمَدَانِيَّةً أُسَكِّنُ بِهَا مُتَحَرَّكَ قُدْرَتِكَ حَتَّى يَتَحَرَّكَ لِي كُلُّ سَاكِنٍ وَيَسْكُنُ لِي كُلُّ مُتَحَرِّكْ، فَأَجِدْنِي قِبْلَةَ كُلِّ مُتَوَجِّهٍ وَجَامِعَ شَمْلِ كُلِّ مُتَفَرِّقٍ مِنْ حَيْثُ اسْمِكَ الَّذِي تَوَجَّهَتْ إِلَيْهِ وُجْهَتِي وَاضْمَحَلَّتْ عِنْدَهُ كَلِمَتِي فَيَقْتَبِسَ كُلُّ مِنِّي جَذْوَةَ هُدًى تُوَضِّحُ لَهُ مَا أَمَّ إِمَامُهُ سَيِّدِنَا مُحَمَّدٌ الفَرْدُ الَّذِي لَوْلَاهُ لَمْ تَثْبُتْ إِبَانَةُ القَبَسِ لِمُوسَى عَلَيْهِ السَّلَامْ.

an tahaba lī ṣamadāniyyatan usakkinu bihā mutaḥarraka qudratika ḥattā yataḥarraka lī kullu sākinin wa yaskunu lī kullu mutaḥarrik, fa-ajidnī qiblata kulli mutawajjihin wa jāmiʿa shamli kulli mutafarriqin min ḥaythu Ismika al-ladhī tawajjahat ilayhi wujhatī wa-ḍmaḥallat ʿindahu kalimatī fa-yaqtabisu kullun minnī jadhwata hudan tuwaḍḍiḥu lahu mā amma imāmuhu sayyidinā Muḥammadunu-l-fardu al-ladhī lawlāhu lam tathbut ibānatu-l-qabasi li-Mūsā ʿalayhi-s-salām.

that You gift me an endurance through which I can calm Your Moving Power, so that every still thing moves, and every moving thing stands still for me. Then, I can find myself as the direction of all destinations and the gatherer of the parts of every dispersed thing, from the vantage of Your Name to which my direction faces and at which my word has been effaced. Then, all can receive from my niche an ember of guidance to clarify what their leader, our master Muhammad ﷺ the unique, has intended.

He without whom the elucidation of Moses ﷺ would not be established.

يَا مَنْ هُوَ هُوَ يَا هُوَ وَلَا أَنَا أَسْأَلُكَ بِكُلِّ اسْمٍ اسْتُمِدَّ بِهِ مِنْ أَلِفِ الغَيْبِ المُحِيطِ بِحَقِيقَةِ كُلِّ مَشْهُودٍ أَنْ تُشْهِدَنِي وَحْدَةَ كُلِّ مُتَكَثِّرٍ فِي بَاطِنِ حَقٍّ وَكَثْرَةَ كُلِّ مُتَوَحِّدٍ فِي ظَاهِرِ كُلِّ حَقِيقَةٍ ثُمَّ وَحْدَةَ الظَّاهِرِ وَالبَاطِنِ حَتَّى لَا يَخْفَى عَلَيَّ غَيْبُ ظَاهِرٍ وَلَا يَغِيبُ عَنِّي خَفِيُّ بَاطِنٍ

yā man Huwa Huwa yā Huwa wa lā anā asʾaluka bi-kulli ismin istumidda bihi min alifi-l-ghaybi-l-muḥīṭi bi-ḥaqīqati kulli mashhūdin an tushhidanī waḥdata kulli mutakaththirin fī bāṭini ḥaqqin wa kathrata kulli mutawaḥḥidin fī ẓāhiri kulli ḥaqīqatin thumma waḥdata-ẓ-ẓāhiri wa-l-bāṭini ḥattā lā yakhfā ʿalayya ghaybu ẓāhirin wa lā yaghību ʿannī khafiyyu bāṭinin

Oh You who is He, He oh He and not me, I ask You with every Name through which providence has been sought from the Alif of the unseen that surrounds the reality of every witnessed thing, that You let me witness the unity of every multiplied thing in the inward of truth and the multitude of every unified thing in the outward of every reality, then also the unity of the outward and inward so that no inner reality of an outward is hidden from me nor any hidden inward is lost from me.

وَأَنْ تُشْهِدَنِي الكُلَّ فِي الكُلِّ يَا مِنْ بِيَدِهِ مَلَكُوتِ كُلِّ شَيْءٍ إِنَّكَ أَنْتَ

أَنْتَ ﴿قُلِ اللهُ ثُمَّ ذَرْهُمْ فِي خَوْضِهِمْ يَلْعَبُونَ﴾[47] ﴿الم * اللهُ لَا إِلَٰهَ إِلَّا هُوَ الحيُّ القَيُّومُ﴾[48] ﴿لَا تَأْخُذُهُ سِنَةٌ وَلَا نَوْمٌ﴾[49]، سَيِّدِي سَلَامٌ عَلَيْكَ أَنْتَ سَنَدِي سَوَاءٌ عِنْدَكَ سِرِّي وَجَهْرِي، تَسْمَعُ نِدَائِي وَتُجِيبُ دُعَائِي. مَحَوْتَ بِنُورِكَ ظُلْمَتِي وَأَحْيَيْتَ بِرُوحِكَ مَيِّتِي

wa an tushhidani-l-kulla fi-l-kulli yā man bi-yadihi malakūti kulli shayʾin innaka Anta Anta "Qul Allāh thumma dharhum fī khawḍihim yalʿabūn" "Alif Lāām Mīīm. Allāhu lā ilāha illā Huwa-l-Ḥayyu-l-Qayyūm" "Lā taʾkhudhuhu sinatun wa lā nawm" Sayyidī salāmun ʿalayka Anta sanadī sawāʾun ʿindaka sirrī wa jahrī, tasmaʿu nidāʾi wa tujību duʿāʾī. maḥawta bi-Nūrika ẓulmatī wa aḥyayta bi-Rūḥika mayyitī

And that You let me witness everything in everything, oh You in whose Hands is the dominion of all things: "Say Allah, then let them be in their toils playing" "Alim Lam Meem. Allah there is no god but He the Eternally Living the Self-Standing" "Neither slumber nor sleep overtakes Him" My master, peace be to You, You are my support. My spoken and unspoken thoughts are the same to You, You hear my call and respond to my supplications. You have erased through Your Light my darkness and enlivened with Your Spirit my dead.

---

47 الأنعام 91

48 آل عمران 1–2

49 البقرة 255

فَأَنْتَ رَبِّي وَبِيَدِكَ سَمْعِي وَبَصَرِي وَقَلْبِي. مَلَكْتَ جَمِيعِي وَشَرَّفْتَ
وَضِيعِي وَأَعْلَيْتَ قَدْرِي وَرَفَعْتَ ذِكْرِي. تَبَارَكْتَ
وَتَعَالَيْتَ نُورَ الأَنْوَارِ وَكَاشِفَ الأَسْرَارِ وَوَاهِبَ الأَعْمَارِ وَمُسْبِلَ
الأَسْتَارْ، وَتَنَزَّهْتَ فِي سُمُوِّ جَلَالِكَ عَنْ سِمَاتِ الْمُحْدَثَاتِ وَعَلَتْ
رُتْبَةُ كَمَالِكَ عَنْ التَّطَرُّقِ إِلَيْهَا بِالشَّهَوَاتِ وَالنَّقَائِصِ وَالآفَاتِ
وَأَنَارَتْ بِشُهُودِ ذَاتِكَ الأَرَضُونَ وَالسَّمَوَاتْ.

fa-anta Rabbī wa bi-Yadika samʿī wa baṣarī wa qalbī. malakta jamīʿī wa sharrafta waḍīʿī wa aʿlayta qadrī wa rafaʿta dhikrī. tabarakta wa taʿālayta Nūra-l-anwāri wa Kāshifa-l-asrāri wa Wāhiba-l-aʿmāri wa Musbila-l-astār, wa tanazzahta fī sumuwwi jalālika ʿan simāti-l-muḥdathāti wa ʿalat rutbatu kamālika ʿani-t-taṭarruqi ilayhā bi-sh-shahawāti wa-n-naqāʾiṣi wa-l-āfāti wa anārat bi-shuhūdi dhātika-l-araḍūna wa-s-samāwāt.

You are my Lord, in Your Hand is my hearing, sight and heart. You have owned my entirety, honored by humbleness, elevated my worth and raised my remembrance. May You be Blessed and Elevated oh Light of lights, Revealer of secrets, Granter of lives and Revealer of concealments. You have transcended, in the loftiness of Your Majesty, the traits of accidents. The rank of Your Perfection is elevated from being reached by lowly desires, shortcomings, and illnesses. The earths and heavens have illumined by witnessing Your Essence.

لَكَ الْمَجْدُ الْأَرْفَعُ وَالْجَنَابُ الْأَوْسَعُ وَالْعِزُّ الْأَمْنَعُ. سُبُّوحٌ قُدُّوسٌ رَبُّ الْمَلَائِكَةِ وَالرُّوحِ. مُنَوِّرُ الصَّيَاصِي الْمُظْلِمَةِ وَغَوَاسِقِ الْهَوَاجِرِ الْمُبْهَمَةِ وَمُنْقِذُ الْغَرْقَى فِي بَحْرِ الْهَوَى. أَعُوذُ بِكَ مِنْ غَاسِقٍ إِذَا وَقَبَ وَحَاسِدٍ إِذَا حَسَدَ وَارْتَقَبَ.

laka-l-majdu-l-arfaʿu wa-l-janābu-l-awsaʿu wa-l-ʿizzu-l-amnaʿ. Subbūḥun Quddūsun Rabbu-l-malāʾikati wa-r-rūḥ. Munawwiru-ṣ-ṣayāṣi-l-muẓlimati wa ghawāsiqi-l-hawājiri-l-mubhamati wa Munqidhu-l-gharqā fī baḥri-l-hawā. aʿūdhu bika min ghāsiqin idhā waqaba wa ḥāsidin idhā ḥasada wa-rtaqab.

To You belongs the Loftiest Nobility, Most Expansive Title, and Impenetrable Exaltation. Most-Glorified and Most-Sanctified, the Lord of angels and spirit. The Illuminator of darkened fortresses, unknown darknesses of heat, and Savior of those drowning in the ocean of desire. I seek refuge in You from the night when it darkens and the envious if they show envy and connivance.

مَلِيكِي أُنَاجِيكَ مُنَاجَاتِ عَبْدٍ كَسِيرٍ، يَعْلَمُ أَنَّكَ تَسْمَعُ وَيَعْتَقِدُ أَنَّكَ تُجِيبُ، وَاقِفًا بِبَابِكَ وُقُوفَ مُضْطَرٍّ لَا يَجِدُ مِنْ دُونِكَ وَكِيلًا. أَسْأَلُكَ اللَّهُمَّ بِاسْمِكَ الَّذِي أَفَضْتَ بِهِ الْخَيْرَاتِ وَأَنْزَلْتَ بِهِ الْبَرَكَاتِ وَمَنَحْتَ بِهِ أَهْلَ الشُّكْرِ الزِّيَادَاتِ وَأَخْرَجْتَ بِهِ مِنَ الظُّلُمَاتِ

Malīkī unājīka munājāti ʿabdin kasīrin, yaʿlamu annaka tasmaʿu wa yaʿtaqidu annaka tujīb, wāqifan bi-bābika *wuqūfa muḍṭṭarin lā yajidu min dūnika wakīla. as᾿aluka Allāhumma bi-Ismika al-ladhī afaḍta bihi-l-khayrāti wa anzalta bihi-l-barakāti wa manaḥta bihi ahla-sh-shukri-z-ziyādāti wa akhrajta bihi mina-ẓ-ẓulumāti*

My Owner, I confide in You the confidence of a broken servant who knows that You hear and believes You will respond, standing at Your Door the standing of one in need who has no guardian other than You. I ask You, oh Allah, by Your Name through which You have overflowed goodness, brought down blessings, granted the people of gratitude abundance and brought out from the darknesses.

أَنْ تُفِيضَ عَلَيَّ مِنْ مَلَابِسِ أَنْوَارِكَ مَا تَرُدُّ بِهِ عَنِّي أَبْصَارَ الأَعَادِي خَاسِرَةً وَأَيْدِيهِمْ قَاصِرَة. وَاجْعَل حَظِّي مِنْكَ إِشْرَاقًا يَجْلُو لِي كُلَّ أَمْرٍ خَفِيٍّ وَيَكْشِفُ لِي عَنْ كُلِّ سِرٍّ عَلِيٍّ وَيَحْرِقُ كُلَّ شَيْطَانٍ غَوِيّ. يَا نُورَ النُّورِ يَا كَاشِفَ كُلِّ مَسْتُورٍ إِلَيْكَ تُرْجَعُ الأُمُورُ وَبِكَ تُدْفَعُ الشُّرُورْ.

an tufīḍa ʿalayya min malābisi anwārika mā taruddu bihi ʿanni abṣāra-l-aʿādī khāsiratan wa aydīhim qāṣirah. wa-jʿal ḥaẓẓī minka ishrāqan yajlū lī kulla amrin khafiyyin wa yakshifu lī ʿan kulli sirrin ʿaliyyin wa yaḥriqu kulla shayṭānin ghawiyy. yā Nūra-l-nūri yā Kāshifa kulli mastūrin ilayka turjaʿu-l-umūru wa bika tudfaʿu-sh-shurūr.

That You unfurl upon me from the garments of Your Lights through which You deter from me the gazes of enemies in loss and their hands in shortcoming. Make my share from You an illumination that clarifies for me every hidden affair, unveils for me every lofty secret, and burns every transgressive devil. Oh, Light of light, Revealer of every hidden thing, to You are affairs returned and through You are evils repelled.

يَا رَبُّ يَا رَحِيمُ يَا غَفُورْ، وَصَلَّى اللهُ عَلَى سَيِّدِنَا مُحَمَّدٍ وَآلِهِ وَصَحْبِهِ أَجْمَعِينْ، وَسَلَامٌ عَلَى الْمُرْسَلِينَ وَالْحَمْدُ للهِ رَبِّ الْعَالَمِينْ.

yā Rabbu yā Raḥīmu yā Ghafūr, wa ṣallā Allāhu ʿalā sayyidinā Muḥammadin wa ālihi wa ṣaḥbihi ajmaʿīn, wa salāmun ʿala-l-mursalīna wa-l-ḥamdu lillāhi Rabbil-ʿālamīn.

Oh, my Lord, Most-Beneficent and Most-Forgiving. And may Allah send His Prayers upon our master Muhammad ﷺ, his family and companions entirely. Salutations be upon the messengers and all praise is due to Allah the Lord of the worlds.

يَوْمُ الأَرْبُعَاء

Yawmu-l-Arbuʿāʾ

The Day of Wednesday

رَبِّ أَكْرِمْنِي بِشُهُودِ أَنْوَارِ قُدْسِكْ، وَأَيِّدْنِي بِسَطْوَةِ ظُهُورِ أُنْسِكْ، حَتَّى أَتَقَلَّبَ فِي سُبُحَاتِ مَعَارِفِ أَسْمَائِكَ تَقَلُّبًا يُطْلِعُنِي عَلَى أَسْرَارِ ذَرَّاتِ وُجُودِي فِي عَوَالِمِ شُهُودِي لِأُشَاهِدَ بِهَا مَا أَوْدَعْتَهُ فِي عَوَالِمِ الْمُلْكِ وَالْمَلَكُوتِ وَأُعَايِنَ سَرَيَانَ سِرِّ قُدْسِكَ فِي شَوَاهِدِ اللَّاهُوتِ وَالنَّاسُوتِ

Rabbi akrimnī bi-shuhūdi anwāri qudsik, wa ayyidnī bi-saṭwati ẓuhūri unsik, ḥattā ataqallaba fī subuḥāti maʿārifi asmāʾika taqalluban yuṭliʿunī ʿalā asrāri dharrāti wujūdī fī ʿawālimi shuhūdī li-ushāhida bihā mā awdaʿtahu fī ʿawālimi-l-mulki wa-l-malakūti wa uʿāyina sarayāni sirri qudsika fī shawāhidi-l-lāhūti wa-n-nāsūt

Oh my Lord, ennoble me by witnessing the Lights of Your Holiness, and support me with the Reach of manifesting Your Intimacy, so that I may fluctuate between the glorifications of the knowledges of Your Names, a fluctuation that shows me the secrets of my being's atoms in the realms I witness, so that I may witness through it what You have placed in the realms of dominion and spirit, and perceive the permeation of the Secret of Your Holiness in the witnessed Divinity and humanity.

وَعَرِّفْنِي مَعْرِفَةً تَامَّةً وَحِكْمَةً عَامَّةً، حَتَّى لَا يَبْقَى مَعْلُومٌ إِلَّا وَأَطَّلِعَ عَلَى دَقَائِقَ حَقَائِقِهِ الْمُنْبَسِطَةُ فِي الْمَوْجُودَاتِ، وَأَدْفَعُ بِهَا ظُلْمَةَ الْأَكْوَانِ الْمَانِعَةِ عَنْ إِدْرَاكِ حَقَائِقِ الْآيَاتِ، وَأَتَصَرَّفُ بِهَا فِي الْقُلُوبِ وَالْأَرْوَاحِ بِمُهَيِّجَاتِ الْمَحَبَّةِ وَالْوِدَادِ وَالرُّشْدِ وَالرَّشَادِ إِنَّكَ أَنْتَ الْمُحِبُّ الْمَحْبُوبُ وَالطَّالِبُ الْمَطْلُوبُ

wa ʿarrifnī maʿrifatan tāmmatan wa ḥikmatan ʿāmmah, ḥattā lā yabqā maʿlūmun illā wa aṭṭaliʿa ʿalā daqāʾiqa ḥaqāʾiqahu-l-munbasiṭatu fi-l-mawjūdāt, wa adfaʿu bihā ẓulmata-l-akwāni-l-māniʿati ʿan idrāki ḥaqāʾiqi-l-āyāt, wa ataṣarrafu bihā fi-l-qulūbi wa-l-arwāḥi bi-muhayyijāti-l-maḥabbati wa-l-widādi wa-r-rushdi wa-r-rashādi innaka Anta-l-Muḥibbu-l-Maḥbūbu wa-ṭ-Ṭālibu-l-Maṭlūb

Acquaint me completely with a perfect wisdom, so that there remains no known thing save that I perceive its minute realities spread in all existent things and repel through it the darkness of universes that deters from comprehending the realities of signs, and I command through it hearts and spirits with the ecstasies of love and desire, maturity, and reasonableness. Indeed, You are the Lover and Beloved, Seeker and Sought-After

يَا مُقَلِّبَ الْقُلُوبِ يَا كَاشِفَ الْكُرُوبِ، وَأَنْتَ عَلَّامُ الْغُيُوبِ سَتَّارُ الْعُيُوبِ غَفَّارُ الذُّنُوبِ، يَا مَنْ لَمْ يَزَلْ سَتَّارًا وَيَا مَنْ لَمْ يَزَلْ غَفَّارًا، يَا غَفَّارُ يَا سَتَّارُ يَا حَفِيظُ يَا وَافِي يَا دَافِعُ يَا مُحْسِنُ يَا عَطُوفُ يَا رَؤُوفُ

يَا عَزِيزُ يَا سَلَامْ. اغْفِرْ لِي وَاسْتُرْنِي وَاحْفَظْنِي وَقِنِي وَادْفَعْ عَنِّي وَأَحْسِنْ إِلَيَّ وَتَعَطَّفْ عَلَيَّ

yā Muqalliba-l-qulūbi yā Kāshifa-l-kurūb, wa anta ʿAllāmu-l-ghuyūbi Sattāru-l-ʿuyūbi Ghaffāru-dh-dhunūb, yā man lam yazal Sattāran wa yā man lam yazal Ghaffara, yā Ghaffaru yā Sattāru yā Ḥafīḍu yā Wāfī yā Dāfiʿu yā Muḥsinu yā ʿAṭūfu yā Raʾūfu yā ʿAzīzu yā Salām. ighfir lī wa-sturnī wa-ḥfaẓnī wa qinī wa-dfaʿ ʿannī wa aḥsin ilayya wa taʿaṭṭaf ʿalayya

Oh, Turner of hearts and Lifter of calamities. You are the Knower of the unseen, Concealer of faults and Forgiver of sins. Oh, You who still Conceals and Forgives. Oh Forgiver, Concealer, Protector, Loyal, Repeller, Bountiful, Clement, Gentle, Exalted and Peace. Forgive, conceal, protect, preserve, and repel and grant me from Your bounties and show me Your Clemency

وَارْأَفْ وَاعْطُفْ، وَاعِزَّنِي وَسَلِّمْنِي وَلَا تُؤَاخِذْنِي بِقَبِيحِ أَفْعَالِي، وَلَا تُجَازِنِي بِسُوءِ أَعْمَالِي، وَتَدَارَكْنِي عَاجِلًا وَآجِلًا بِلُطْفِكَ التَّامِّ وَخَلِّصْنِي بِخَالِصِ رَحْمَتِكَ وَلَا تُحْوِجْنِي إِلَى أَحَدٍ سِوَاكَ وَعَافِنِي وَاعْفُ عَنِّي وَأَصْلِحْ لِي شَأْنِي كُلَّه

wa-rʾaf wa-ʿṭuf, wa aʿizzanī wa sallimnī wa lā tuʾākhidhnī bi-qabīḥi afʿālī, wa lā tujāzinī bi-sūʾi aʿmālī, wa tadāraknī ʿājilan wa ājilan bi-luṭfika-t-tāmmi wa khalliṣnī bi-khāliṣi raḥmatika wa lā tuḥwijnī ilā aḥadin siwāka wa ʿāfinī wa-ʿfu ʿannī wa aṣliḥ lī shaʾnī kullah

Be Gentle and Clement, exalt me and grant me safety. Do not judge me by my ugly deeds, and do not recompense me with the evil in my deeds. Restore me, now and then, with Your Complete Clemency, and purify me with Your Purest Mercy. Do not leave me for anyone other than You. Recuperate and forgive me, rectify my entire affair

يَا لَا إِلَهَ إِلَّا أَنْتَ سُبْحَانَكَ إِنِّي كُنْتُ مِنَ الظَّالِمِينْ، وَأَنْتَ أَرْحَمُ الرَّاحِمِينْ، وَصَلَّى اللهُ عَلَى سَيِّدِنَا مُحَمَّدٍ وَعَلَى آلِهِ وَأَصْحَابِهِ أَجْمَعِينْ، وَسَلَامٌ عَلَى الْمُرْسَلِينْ، وَالْحَمْدُ للهِ رَبِّ الْعَالَمِينْ.

yā lā ilāha illā Anta subḥānaka innī kuntu mina-ẓ-ẓālimīn, wa Anta Arḥamu-r-rāḥimīn, wa ṣallā Allāhu ʿalā sayyidinā Muḥammadin wa ʿalā ālihi wa aṣḥābihi ajmaʿīn, wa salāmun ʿala-l-mursalīn, wa-l-ḥamdu lillāhi Rabbi-l-ʿālamīn.

Oh 'there is no god but You,' Glory be to You. Indeed, I have been from the transgressors, while You are the Most Merciful of the merciful. May Allah send His Prayers upon our master Muhammad ﷺ, his family and companions entirely. Salutations be upon the messengers, and all praise is due to Allah the Lord of the worlds.

لَيْلَةُ الخَمِيس

Laylatu-l-Khamīs
The Night of Thursday

سَيِّدِي أَنْتَ مُسَبِّبُ الأَسْبَابِ وَمُرَتِّبُهَا، وَمُصَرِّفُ القُلُوبِ وَمُقَلِّبُهَا، أَسْأَلُكَ بِالحِكْمَةِ الَّتِي اقْتَضَتْ تَرْتِيبَ الأَسْبَابِ الأَوَّلِ وَتَأْثِيرِ الأَعْلَى فِي الأَسْفَلْ، أَنْ تُشْهِدَنِي تَرْتِيبَ الأَسْبَابِ صُعُودًا وَنُزُولًا حَتَّى أَشْهَدَ مِنْكَ البَاطِنَ فِي الظَّاهِرِ وَالظَّاهِرَ فِي البَاطِنِ مِنْهَا بِشُهُودِ الظَّاهِرِ وَالأَوَّلَ غَيْرَ الآخِرْ

Sayyidī Anta Musabbibu-l-asbābi wa Murattibuhā, wa Muṣarrifu-l-qulūbi wa muqallibuhā, as'aluka bi-l-ḥikmati al-latī iqtaḍat tartībi-l-asbābi-l-awwali wa ta'thīri-l-a'lā fi-l-asfal, an tushhidanī tartība-l-asbābi ṣu'ūdan wa nuzūlan ḥattā ashhada minka-l-bāṭina fi-ẓ-ẓāhiri wa-ẓ-ẓāhira fi-l-bāṭini minhā bi-shuhūdi-ẓ-ẓāhiri wa-l-awwala ghayra-l-ākhir

My Master, You are the Causer of causes and its Arranger, the Commander of hearts and their Turner. I ask You by the wisdom that demands the arrangement of causes, beginning with the first, and the effect of the highest on the lowest, that You let me witness the arrangement of causes, in ascent and descent so that I may witness among them, from You, the inward in the outward and outward in inward, through witnessing the outward and first as other than the last

وَأَلْحَظَ حِكْمَةَ التَّرْتِيبِ بِشُهودِ المَرَتِّبْ، وَمُسَبِّبَ الأَسْبابِ مَسْبُوقًا بِالْمُسَبِّبْ، فَلا أُحْجَبَ عَنْ العَيْنِ بِالغَيْنْ. إِلَهي أَنِلْني مِفْتاحَ الإِذْنِ الَّذي هُوَ كافُ المَعارِفِ حَتَّى أَنْطِقَ فِي كُلِّ بِدايَةٍ بِإِسْمِكَ البَديعِ الَّذي افْتَتَحْتَ بِهِ كُلَّ رَقِيمٍ مَسْطُورْ. يا مَنْ بِسُمُوِّ أَسْمائِهِ يَنْخَفِضُ كُلُّ مُتَعالْ

wa alḥaẓa ḥikmata-t-tartībi bi-shuhūdi-l-Murattib, wa Musabbiba-l-asbābi masbūqan bi-l-Musabbib, fa-lā uḥjaba ʿani-l-ʿayni bi-l-ghayn. Ilāhī anilnī miftāḥa-l-idhni al-ladhī huwa kāfu-l-maʿārifi ḥattā anṭiqa fī kulli bidāyatin bi-ismika-l-Badīʿi-l-ladhī iftataḥta bihi kulla raqīmin masṭūr. yā man bi-sumuwwi asmāʾihi yankhafiḍu kullu mutaʿāl

And so that I perceive the wisdom of arrangement by witnessing the Arranger, and the Causer of Causes preceded by the Prime Causer. Then, I will not be veiled by the fog from the Essence. Oh Allah, gift me Your Permission's key, which is the Kaf of gnoses, so that I may utter, in every beginning, Your Name the Innovator, through which You have begun every written tablet. Oh You, through whose Lofty Names every arrogant is humbled

وَكُلٌّ بِكَ وَأَنْتَ بِلا نَحْنْ، وَأَنْتَ مُبْدِعُ كُلِّ شَيْءٍ وَبادِيهِ لَكَ الحَمْدُ عَلَى كُلِّ بِدايَةْ ، وَلَكَ الشُّكْرُ يا باقِي عَلَى كُلِّ نِهايَة، أَنْتَ الباعِثُ عَلَى كُلِّ خَيْرٍ باطِنِ الأُمُورْ، يا باسِطَ الرِّزْقَ لِلعالَمِينَ بارِكْ اللهُمَّ عَلَيَّ فِي

الآخِرِينَ كَمَا بَارَكْتَ عَلَى سَيِّدِنَا مُحَمَّدٍ وَإِبْرَاهِيمَ إِنَّهُ مِنْكَ وَإِلَيْكَ وَإِنَّهُ

بِسْمِ اللهِ الرَّحْمَنِ الرَّحِيمْ

wa kullun bika wa Anta bi-lā naḥn, wa Anta mubdiʿu kulla shayʾin wa bādīhi laka-l-ḥamdu ʿalā kulli bidāyah, wa laka-sh-shukru yā Bāqī ʿalā kulli nihāyah, Anta-l-Bāʿithu ʿalā kulli khayri bāṭini-l-umūr, yā Bāṣiṭa-r-rizqa li-l-ʿālamīna bārik Allāhumma ʿalayya fi-l-ākhirīna ka-mā bārakta ʿalā sayyidinā Muḥammadin wa Ibrāhīma innahu minka wa ilayka wa innahu bismillāhi-r-Raḥmāni-r-Raḥīm

All is through You, yet You are not through us. You are the Innovator of everything and its Beginner. All praise is due to You for every beginning, and gratitude is due to You, oh Subsistent One, for every end. You are the Resurrector, upon every goodness, in the inward of affairs. Oh, Spreader of sustenance for creation, bless me, oh Allah, in the lasts as You have blessed our masters Muhammad ﷺ and Ibrahim عليه السلام. Indeed, he is from and to You and he/it[50] is 'in the Name of Allah, Most-Merciful Most-Beneficent'

﴿بَدِيعُ السَّمَوٰتِ وَالأَرْضِ وَإِذَا قَضَى أَمْرًا فَإِنَّمَا يَقُولُ لَهُ كُنْ فَيَكُونْ﴾[51] إِلَهِي أَنْتَ الثَّابِتُ قَبْلَ كُلِّ ثَابِتٍ وَالبَاقِي بَعْدَ كُلِّ صَامِتٍ

---

[50] The ambivalent use of the indefinite emphatic pronoun *innahu* [indeed he/it is], as well as *huwa* [he/it is], is always used by the Shaykh to connote multiple meanings at once: Allah ﷻ, Prophet Muhammad ﷺ and the Qurʾān.

[51] البقرة 117

وَنَاطِقٍ، لَا إِلَهَ إِلَّا أَنْتَ وَلَا مَوْجُودٌ سِوَاكَ. لَكَ الْكِبْرِيَاءُ وَالْجَبَرُوتُ وَالْعَظَمَةُ وَالْمَلَكُوتْ. تَقْهَرُ الْجَبَّارِينَ وَتُبِيدُ كَيْدَ الظَّالِمِينْ، وَتُبَدِّدُ شَمْلَ الْمُلْحِدِينْ، وَتُذِلُّ رِقَابَ الْمُتَكَبِّرِينْ

"Badīʿu-s-samāwāti wa-l-arḍi wa idhā qaḍā amran fa-innamā yaqūlu lahu kun fa-yakūn" Ilāhī Anta-th-Thābitu qabla kulli thābitin wa-l-Bāqī baʿda kulli ṣāmitin wa nāṭiq, lā ilāha illā Anta wa lā mawjūdun siwāk. laka-l-kibriyāʾu wa-l-jabarūtu wa-l-ʿaẓamatu wa-l-malakūt. taqharu-l-jabbārīna wa tubīdu kayda-ẓ-ẓālimīn, wa tubaddida shamla-l-mulḥidīn, wa tudhillu riqāba-l-mutakabbirīn

"The Innovator of the heavens and earth, if He wills an affair, He merely says to it: 'Be' and it will be" Oh Allah, You are the Immutable before every immutable and the Remaining One after every silent and speaking thing. There is no god but You and there is no existent but You. To You belongs Pride and Might, Greatness, and Dominion. You subdue the transgressors, eradicate the connivance of oppressors, disperse the unity of disbelievers, and humiliate the necks of arrogant ones

أَسْأَلُكَ يَا غَالِبَ كُلِّ غَالِبٍ وَيَا مُدْرِكَ كُلِّ هَارِبْ، بِرِدَاءِ كِبْرِيَائِكَ وَإِزَارِ عَظَمَتِكَ وَسُرَادِقَاتِ هَيْبَتِكَ وَبِمَا وَرَاءَ ذَلِكَ كُلِّهِ بِمَا لَا يَعْلَمُهُ إِلَّا أَنْتَ

asʾaluka yā Ghāliba kulli ghālibin wa yā Mudrika kulli hārib, bi-ridāʾi kibriyāʾika wa izāri ʿaẓamatika wa surādiqāti haybatika wa bi-mā warā'a dhālika kullihi bi-mā lā yaʿlamuhu illā Anta

I ask You, oh Defeater of every defeater and Catcher of every runner, by the garment of Your Pride, cloth of Your Greatness, treasuries of Your Awe and what is beyond all of these, what only You know

أَنْ تَكْسُوَنِي هَيْبَةً مِنْ هَيْبَتِكَ تَخْضَعُ لَهَا الْقُلُوبُ وَتَخْشَعُ لَهَا الْأَبْصَارُ، وَمَلِّكْنِي نَاصِيَةَ كُلِّ مَنْ نَاصِيَتُهُ بِيَدِكْ. وَأَبْقِ عَلَيَّ ذُلَّ الْعُبُودِيَّةِ فِي ذَلِكَ كُلِّهْ

an taksuwanī haybatan min haybatika takhḍaʿu laha-l-qulūbu wa takhshaʿu laha-l-abṣār, wa mallikni nāṣiyata kulli man nāṣiyatuhu bi-yadik. wa abqi ʿalayya dhulla-l-ʿubūdiyyati fī dhālika kullih

That You cover me with an awe from Your Awe to which hearts submit and gazes lowered and grant me dominion over the forelocks of all those whose forelocks are in Your Hand and maintain for me the humility of servanthood in all of this

وَاعْصِمْنِي مِنَ الزَّلَلْ، وَأَيِّدْنِي فِي الْقَوْلِ وَالْعَمَلْ، أَنْتَ أَنْتَ مُثَبِّتُ الْقُلُوبِ وَكَاشِفُ الْكُرُوبِ، لَا إِلَهَ إِلَّا أَنْتَ، وَصَلَّى اللهُ عَلَى سَيِّدِنَا مُحَمَّدٍ وَآلِهِ وَصَحْبِهِ أَجْمَعِينْ، وَالْحَمْدُ للهِ رَبِّ الْعَالَمِينْ.

wa-ʿṣimnī mina-z-zalal, wa ayyidnī fi-l-qawli wa-l-ʿamal, Anta Anta Muthabbitu-l-qulūbi wa Kāshifu-l-kurūb, lā ilāha illā Ant, wa ṣallā Allāhu ʿalā sayyidinā Muḥammadin wa ālihi wa ṣaḥbihi ajmaʿīn, wa-l-ḥamdu lillāhi Rabbil ʿālamīn.

Guard me from mistakes, support me in speech and action. Indeed, it is You who is the Affirmer of hearts and Lifter of calamities. There is no god but You, and may Allah send His Prayers upon our master Muhammad ﷺ, his family and companions entirely. All praise is due to Allah the Lord of the worlds.

يَوْمُ الخَمِيسْ

Yawmu-l-Khamīs

The Day of Thursday

إِلَهِي أَنْتَ القَائِمُ بِذَاتِكَ وَالمُحِيطُ بِصِفَاتِكْ، وَالمُتَجَلِّي بِأَسْمَائِكَ وَالظَّاهِرُ بِأَفْعَالِكَ وَالبَاطِنُ بِمَا لَا يَعْلَمُهُ إِلَّا أَنْتْ. تَوَحَّدْتَ فِي جَلَالِكَ فَأَنْتَ الوَاحِدُ الأَحَدْ، وَتَفَرَّدْتَ بِالبَقَاءِ فِي الأَزَلِ وَالأَبَدْ. أَنْتَ اللهُ المُتَفَرِّدُ بِالوَحْدَانِيَّةِ فِي إِيَّاكَ لَا مَعَكَ غَيْرُكَ وَلَا فِيكَ سِوَاكْ.

Ilāhī Anta-l-Qāʾimu bi-dhātika wa-l-Muḥīṭu bi-ṣifātik, wa-l-Mutajallī bi-asmāʾika wa-Ẓāhiru bi-afʿālika wa-l-Bāṭinu bi-mā lā yaʿlamuhu illā Ant. tawaḥḥadta fī jalālika fa-Anta-l-Wāḥidu-l-Aḥad, wa tafarradta bi-l-baqāʾi fi-l-azali wa-l-abad. Anta Allāhu-l-Mutafarridu bi-l-waḥdāniyyati fī Iyyāka lā maʿaka ghayruka wa lā fīka siwāk.

Oh Allah, You are the Self-Standing through Your Essence, Encompassing through Your Attributes, Manifesting through Your Names, Outward through Your Actions and Inward through that which no one knows but You. You are Singular in Your Majesty. Hence, You are the One and Unique. You are Distinguished in Your Subsistence, pre-eternally and eternally. You are Allah, distinguished by oneness in You, there is no other with You, nor another in You.

أَسْأَلُكَ الفَنَاءَ فِي بَقَائِكَ وَالبَقَاءَ بِكَ لَا مَعَكَ لَا إِلَهَ إِلَّا أَنْتْ، إِلَهِي غَيِّبْنِي فِي حُضُورِكَ وَافْنِنِي فِي وُجُودِكَ وَاسْتَهْلِكْنِي فِي شُهُودِكَ

وَاقْطَعْ بَيْنِي وَبَيْنَ الْقَوَاطِعِ الَّتِي تَقْطَعُ بَيْنِي وَبَيْنَكَ، وَاشْغَلْنِي بِالشُّغْلِ بِكَ عَنْ كُلِّ شَاغِلٍ يَشْغَلُنِي عَنْكَ لَا إِلَهَ إِلَّا أَنْتَ

as'aluka-l-fanā'a fī baqā'ika wa-l-baqā'a bika lā ma'aka lā ilāha illā Ant, Ilāhī ghayyibnī fī ḥuḍūrika wa afninī fī wujūdika wa-stahliknī fī shuhūdika wa-qṭa' baynī wa bayna-l-qawāṭi'i-l-latī taqṭa'u baynī wa baynak, wa-shghalnī bi-sh-shughli bika 'an kulli shāghilin yashghalunī 'anka lā ilāha illā Ant

I ask You for annihilation in Your Subsistence and subsisting through, not with, You. There is no god but You. Oh Allah, make me absent in Your Presence, annihilate me in Your Being, consume me in witnessing You, separate between me and the obstacles that stand between me and You. Keep me occupied with You, away from every burden that prevents me from You. There is no god but You

إِلَهِي أَنْتَ الْمَوْجُودُ الْحَقُّ وَأَنَا الْمَعْدُومُ الْأَصْلُ. بَقَاؤُكَ بِالذَّاتِ وَبَقَائِي بِالْعَرَضِ. إِلَهِي فَجُدْ بِوُجُودِكَ الْحَقِّ عَلَى عَدَمِي بِالْأَصْلِ حَتَّى أَكُونَ كَمَا كُنْتُ حَيْثُ لَمْ أَكُنْ وَأَنْتَ كَمَا أَنْتَ حَيْثُ لَمْ تَزَلْ. لَا إِلَهَ إِلَّا أَنْتَ.

إِلَهِي أَنْتَ الْفَعَّالُ لِمَا تُرِيدُ وَأَنَا عَبْدٌ لَكَ مِنْ بَعْضِ الْعَبِيدِ

Ilāhī Anta-l-Mawjūdu-l-Ḥaqqu wa ana-l-ma'dūmu-l-aṣl. baqā'uka bi-dh-dhāti wa baqā'ī bi-l-'araḍ. Ilāhī fa-jud bi-wujūdika-l-ḥaqqi 'alā 'adamī bi-l-aṣli ḥattā akūna ka-mā kuntu ḥaythu lam akun wa Anta ka-mā Anta ḥaythu lam tazal. lā ilāha illā Ant. Ilāhī Anta-l-Fa''ālu li-mā turīdu wa

anā ʿabdun laka min baʿḍi-l-ʿabīd

Oh Allah, You are the Real Being while I am the original non-existent. Your Subsistence is through the Essence, while my subsistence is accidental. Oh Allah, bestow Your Real Being upon my original non-existence so that I be as I have always been, not existent, while You as You are: always Is. There is no god but You. Oh Allah, You are the Fulfiller of Your Will, while I am merely one from among the servants.

إِلَهِي أَرَدْتَنِي وَأَرَدْتَ مِنِّي فَأَنَا الْمُرَادُ وَأَنْتَ الْمُرِيدُ فَكُنْ أَنْتَ مُرَادُكَ مِنِّي حَيْثُ تَكُونُ أَنْتَ الْمُرَادُ وَأَنَا الْمُرِيدُ لَا إِلَهَ إِلَّا أَنْتَ. إِلَهِي أَنْتَ الْبَاطِنُ فِي كُلِّ غَيْبٍ وَالظَّاهِرُ فِي كُلِّ عَيْنٍ وَالْمَسْمُوعُ فِي كُلِّ خَبَرِ صِدْقٍ وَمَيْنٍ، وَالْمَعْلُومُ فِي مَرْتَبَةِ الْوَاحِدِ وَالْإِثْنَيْنِ.

Ilāhī aradtnī wa aradta minnī fa-ana-l-murādu wa Anta-l-Murīdu fa-kun Anta murāduka minnī ḥaythu takūnu Anta-l-Murādu wa ana-l-murīd lā ilāha illā Ant. Ilāhī Anta-l-Bāṭinu fī kulli ghaybin wa-ẓ-Ẓāhiru fī kulli ʿaynin wa-l-Masmūʿu fī kulli khabari ṣidqin wa mayn, wa-l-Maʿlūmu fī martabati-l-wāḥidi wa-l-ithnayn.

Oh Allah, You willed me and from me. Thus, I am the sought after and You are the Seeker. So let Your will for me be such that You are the Sought After and I am the seeker. There is no god but You. Oh Allah, You are the Inward in every unseen and Outward in every essence, He who is Heard in every news of truth and falsehood, and what is Known in the rank of singularity and duality.

تَسَمَّيْتَ بِأَسْمَاءِ النُّزُولِ وَاحْتَجَبْتَ عَنْ لَوَاحِظِ العُيُونْ، وَاخْتَفَيْتَ عَنْ مَدَارِكِ العُقُولْ. إِلَهِي تَجَلَّيْتَ بِخَصَائِصِ تَجَلِّيَاتِ الصِّفَاتِ فَتَعَيَّنْتَ فِي مَرَاتِبِ المَوْجُودَاتْ، وَتَسَمَّيْتَ فِي كُلِّ مَرْتَبَةٍ بِحَقَائِقِ المُسَمَّيَاتْ، وَنَصَبْتَ شَوَاهِدَ العُقُولِ عَلَى دَقَائِقِ حَقَائِقِ الآيَاتِ وَغُيُوبِ المَعْلُومَاتْ

tasammayta bi-asmāʾi-n-nuzūli wa-ḥtajabta ʿan lawāḥiẓi-l-ʿuyūn, wa-khtafayta ʿan madāriki-l-ʿuqūl. Ilāhī tajallayta bi-khaṣāʾiṣi tajalliyāti-ṣ-ṣifāti fa-taʿayyanta fī marātibi-l-mawjūdāt, wa tasamayyta fī kulli martabatin bi-ḥaqāʾiqi-l-musammayāt, wa naṣabta shawāhidi-l-ʿuqūli ʿalā daqāʾiqi ḥaqāʾiqi-l-āyāti wa ghuyūbi-l-maʿlūmāt

You are Named by the names of descent, Veiled from the perception of eyes, and hidden from the comprehension of intellects. Oh Allah, You Manifested through the specifics of manifestations of attributes, whence You were Identified in the ranks of existent things. You are Named in every rank by the realities of named things. You established the witnesses of intellects upon the detailed realities of signs and unseen known things.

وَأَطْلَقْتَ سَوَابِقَ الأَرْوَاحِ فِي مَيَادِينِ المَعَارِفِ الإِلَهِيَّةِ فَحَارَتْ ثُمَّ تَاهَتْ فِي إِشَارَاتِ لَطَائِفِهَا السِّرْيَانِيَّةْ. فَلَمَّا غَيَّبْتَهَا عَنِ الكُلِّيَةِ وَالجُزْئِيَّةِ وَنَقَلْتَهَا عَنْ الآنِيَّةِ وَالأَيْنِيَّة، وَسَلَبْتَهَا عَنْ الكَمِّيَّةِ وَالمَاهِيَّة،

وَتَعَرَّفْتَ لَهَا فِي مَعَارِفِ التَّنْكِيرِ بِالْمَعَارِفِ الذَّاتِيَّة

wa aṭlaqta sawābiqa-l-arwāḥi fī mayādīni-l-maʿārifi-l-ilāhiyyati fa-ḥārat thumma tāhat fī ishārāti laṭāʾifiha-s-siriyāniyyah. fa-lammā ghayyabtahā ʿani-l-kulliyati wa-l-juzʾiyyati wa naqaltahā ʿani-l-āniyyati wa-l-ayniyyah, wa salabtahā ʿani-l-kammiyyati wa-l-māhiyyah, wa taʿarrafta lahā fī maʿārifi-t-tankīri bi-l-maʿārifi-dh-dhātiyyah

Then You sent forth the preceding spirits in the courts of Divine Gnoses, whence they became perplexed and lost amidst the allusions of their Syriac subtleties.[52] Then, when You made them absent in whole and part, moved them away from identity and location, deprived them of quantity and matter and acquainted them to Yourself in the familiarity of indefinity through Essential Gnoses

وَحَرَّرْتَهَا بِمُطَالَعَاتِ الرُّبُوبِيَّةِ فِي الْمَوَاقِفِ الإِلَهِيَّة، وَأَسْقَطْتَ عَنْهَا الْبَيْنَ عِنْدَ رَفْعِ حِجَابِ الْبَيْن، فَانْتَظَمَتْ بِالنِّظَامِ الْقَدِيمِ فِي سِلْكِ بِسْمِ اللهِ الرَّحْمَنِ الرَّحِيمْ. إِلَهِي كَمْ أُنَادِيكَ فِي النَّادِي وَأَنْتَ الْمُنَادِي لِلنَّادِي. وَكَمْ أُنَاجِيكَ بِمُنَاجَاتِ النَّاجِي وَأَنْتَ الْمُنَاجِي لِلنَّاجِي.

wa ḥarrartahā bi-muṭālaʿāti-r-rubūbiyyati fi-l-mawāqifi-l-ilāhiyyah, wa asqaṭta ʿanha-l-bayna ʿinda rafʿi ḥijābi-l-bayn, fa-ntaẓamat bi-n-niẓāmi-l-qadīmi fī silki bismillāhi-r-

---

[52] This can either as siriyāniyyah or suriyāniyyah, as referred to by the Moroccan saint Sidi ʿAbdul ʿAzīz al-Dabbāgh in the *Ibrīz*. No matter the pronunciation, this term refers less so to the human language which is the ancestor of Arabic but the language of the spiritual realm and beings.

Raḥmāni-r-Raḥīm. Ilāhī kam unādīka fi-n-nādī wa Anta-l-Munādī li-n-nādī. wa kam unājīka bi-munājāti-n-nājī wa Anta-l-Munājī li-n-Nājī.

Then You liberated them through readings of Lordship in Divine Events and overlooked their distance when You lifted the veil of in-between, whence they became aligned according to the pre-eternal governance on the occupation of 'In the Name of Allah, Most-Merciful Most-Beneficent.' Oh Allah, how often do I call upon You in associations, while You are the Caller to the caller, and how often do I converse with You, through the soliloquys of a confidant, while You are the Confidant to the confidant.

إِلَهي إِذَا كَانَ الوَصْلُ عَيْنُ القَطْعِ وَالقُرْبُ نَفْسُ البُعْدِ وَالعِلْمُ مَوْضِعُ الجَهْلِ وَالمَعْرِفَةُ مُسْتَقَرُّ التَّنْكِيرِ فَكَيْفَ القَصْدُ وَمِنْ أَيْنَ السَّبِيلْ؟ إِلَهي أَنْتَ المَطْلُوبُ وَرَاءَ كُلِّ قَاصِدٍ وَالإِقْرَارُ فِي عَيْنِ الجَاحِدْ، وَقُرْبُ القُرْبِ فِي الفَرْقِ المُتَبَاعِدْ، وَقَدْ اسْتَوْلَى الوَهْمُ عَلَى الفَهْمِ فَأَيْنَ القَصْدُ وَمَنْ المُتَبَاعِدْ؟

Ilāhī idhā kāna-l-waṣlu ʿaynu-l-qaṭʿi wa-l-qurbu nafsu-l-buʿdi wa-l-ʿilmu mawḍiʿu-l-jahli wa-l-maʿrifatu mustaqarru-t-tankīri fa-kayfa-l-qaṣdu wa min ayna-s-sabīl? Ilāhī Anta-l-Maṭlūbu warāʾa kulli qāṣidin wa-l-iqrāru fī ʿayni-l-jāḥid, wa Qurbu-l-qurbi fi-l-farqi-l-mutabāʿid, wa qadi-stawla-l-wahmu ʿala-l-fahmi fa-ayna-l-qaṣdu wa mani-l-mutabāʿid?

Oh Allah, if connections are identical with disconnections, nearness the same as distance, knowledge the place of ignorance and gnosis the vessel of denial, then whence is intention and where is the way forward? Oh Allah, You are the Sought-After behind every seeker, affirmation in the eye of the denier and the quintessential nearness in increasing distance. Indeed, illusion has overwhelmed comprehension, so where is intention and alienation?

الْحُسْنُ يَقُولُ إِيَّاكَ وَالْقُبْحُ يُنَادِي الَّذِي أَحْسَنَ كُلَّ شَيْءٍ خَلَقَهْ. فَالْأَوَّلُ غَايَةٌ يَقِفُ عِنْدَهَا السَّيْرْ، وَالثَّانِي حِجَابٌ لِحُكْمِ تَوَهُّمِ الْغَيْرْ. إِلَهِي مَتَى يَتَخَلَّصُ الْعَقْلُ عَنْ عِقَالِ الْعَوَائِقِ وَيَلْحَظُ لَوَاحِظَ الْفِكْرِ مِنْ مَحَاسِنِ الْحُسْنَى مِنْ أَعْيُنِ الْحَقَائِقِ وَيَنْفَكُّ الْفَهْمُ عَنْ أَصْلِ الْإِفْكِ

al-ḥusnu yaqūlu Iyyāka wa-l-qubḥu yunādī al-ladhī aḥsana kulla shayʾin khalaqah. fa-l-awwalu ghāyatun yaqifu ʿindaha-s-sayr, wa-th-thānī ḥijābun li-ḥukmi tawahhumi-l-ghayr. Ilāhī matā yatakhallaṣu-l-ʿaqlu ʿan ʿiqāli-l-ʿawāʾiqi wa yalḥaẓu lawāḥiẓa-l-fikri min maḥāsini-l-ḥusnā min aʿyuni-l-ḥaqāʾiqi wa yanfakku-l-fahmu ʿan aṣli-l-ifk

Beauty says: 'You' while ugliness proclaims: 'He is the One who beautified everything He created.' Thus, the first is a destination at which travel halts, while the second is a veil due to the presumption of another.

Oh Allah, when will the intellect be free from the leash of obstacles, the glimpses of reflection perceive the beauties of graciousness in the essences of realities, and comprehension depart from sin?

وَيَتَحَلَّلُ الوَهْمُ مِنْ أَوْصَالِ حِبَالِ أَشْرَاكِ الشِّرْكِ وَيَنْجُو التَّصَوُّرُ مِنْ فِرَقِ الفَرْقِ، وَتَتَجَرَّدُ النَّفْسُ النَّفِيسَةُ عَنْ خُلُقِ أَخْلَاقِ تَخَلُّقَاتِ الخَلْقِ؟ إِلَهِي أَنْتَ لَا تَنْفَعُكَ الطَّاعَاتُ وَلَا تَضُرُّكَ المَعَاصِي وَبِيَدِكَ قَهْرُ سُلْطَانَ مَلَكُوتِ القُلُوبِ وَالنَّوَاصِي. وَإِلَيْكَ يَرْجِعُ الأَمْرُ كُلُّهُ فَلَا نِسْبَةَ لِلطَّائِعِ وَالعَاصِي

wa yataḥallalu-l-wahmu min awṣāli ḥibāli ashrāki-sh-shirki wa yanju-t-taṣawwuru min firaqi-l-farq, wa tatajarradu-n-nafsu-n-nafīsatu ʿan khuluqi akhlāqi takhalluqāti-l-khalq? Ilāhī Anta lā tanfaʿuka-ṭ-ṭāʿātu wa lā taḍarruka-l-maʿāṣī wa bi-yadika qahru sulṭāna malakūti-l-qulūbi wa-n-nawāṣī. wa ilayka yarjiʿu-l-amru kulluhu fa-lā nisbata li-ṭ-ṭāʾiʿi wa-l-ʿāṣī

and [praiseworthy] illusion can be cleansed from links and ropes to the traps of polytheism, imagination can be saved from the tribes of separation and the precious soul can be purified from the manner of embodying creation's traits? Oh Allah, You are neither benefited by obedience nor harmed by disobedience. In Your Hand is the subduing of the authority of the dominion of hearts and forelocks. To You returns the entire affair, whence there is neither share for the obedient nor disobedient

إِلَهِي أَنْتَ لَا يَشْغَلُكَ شَأْنٌ عَنْ شَأْن. إِلَهِي أَنْتَ لَا يَحْصُرُكَ الوُجُوبُ وَلَا يَحُدُّكَ الإِمْكَانُ وَلَا يَحْجُبُكَ الإِبْهَامُ وَلَا يُوَضِّحُكَ البَيَانْ. إِلَهِي أَنْتَ لَا يُرَجِّحُكَ الدَّلِيلُ وَلَا يُحَقِّقُكَ البُرْهَانْ. إِلَهِي أَنْتَ الأَبَدُ وَالأَزَلُ فِي حَقِّكَ سِيَّانْ. إِلَهِي مَا أَنْتَ وَمَا أَنَا وَمَا هُوَ وَمَا هِيَ؟

Ilāhī Anta lā yashghaluka shaʾnun ʿan shaʾn. Ilāhī Anta lā yaḥṣuruka-l-wujūbu wa lā yaḥudduka-l-imkānu wa lā yaḥjubuka-l-ibhāmu wa lā yuwaḍḍiḥuka-l-bayān. Ilāhī Anta lā yurajjiḥuka-d-dalīlu wa lā yuḥaqqiquka-l-burhān. Ilāhī Anta-l-abadu wa-l-azalu fī ḥaqqika siyyān. Ilāhī mā Anta wa mā anā wa mā huwa wa mā hiya?

Oh Allah, You are not preoccupied by one affair from another. Oh Allah, You are not delimited by necessity, limited by possibility, veiled by obscurity nor clarified by eloquence. Oh Allah, You are neither made True by evidence nor actualized by proofs. Oh Allah, both pre-eternity and eternity are the same to You. Oh Allah, who are You, me, him, or her?

إِلَهِي أَفِي الكَثْرَةِ أَطْلُبُكَ أَمْ فِي الوَحْدَةْ؟ وَبِالأَمَدِ أَنْتَظِرُ فَرَجَكَ أَمْ بِالمُدَّةِ؟ فَلَا عُدَّةٌ لِعَبْدٍ دُونَكَ وَلَا عُمْدَةْ. إِلَهِي بَقَائِي بِكَ فِي فَنَائِي عَنِّي أَمْ فِيكَ أَمْ بِكْ؟ وَفَنَائِي كَذَلِكَ مُحَقَّقٌ بِكَ أَمْ مُتَوَهَّمٌ بِي أَمْ بِالعَكْسِ أَمْ هُوَ أَمْرٌ مُشْتَرَكْ وَكَذَلِكَ بَقَائِي فِيكْ؟

Ilāhī a-fi-l-kathrati aṭlubuka am fi-l-waḥdah? wa bi-l-amadi antaẓiru farajaka am bi-l-muddah? fa-lā ʿuddatun li-ʿabdin dūnaka wa lā ʿumdah. Ilāhī baqāʾī bika fī fanāʾī ʿannī am fīka am bik? wa fanāʾī ka-dhālika muḥaqqaqun bika am mutawahhamun bī am bi-l-ʿaksi am huwa amrun mushtarak wa ka-dhālika baqāʾī fīk?

Oh Allah, should I seek You in abundance or unity? Should I await Your Relief at the end or in time? Indeed, there are neither means nor support for a servant without You. Oh Allah, my subsistence through You, is it amidst my annihilation from me, within You or through You? Likewise, is my annihilation realized through You, fantasized through me, the inverse or is it a shared affair, and so for my subsistence in You?

إِلَهِي سُكُوتِي خَرَسٌ يُوجِبُ الصَّمَمْ، وَكَلَامِي صَمَمٌ يُوجِبُ البَكَمْ، وَالحَيْرَةُ فِي كُلِّ ذَلِكَ وَلَا حَيْرَةْ. بِسْمِ اللهِ رَبِّيَ اللهُ، بِسْمِ اللهِ حَسْبِيَ اللهُ، بِسْمِ اللهِ وَبِاللهِ، بِسْمِ اللهِ تَوَكَّلْتُ عَلَى اللهِ، بِسْمِ اللهِ سَأَلْتُ مِنَ اللهِ، بِسْمِ اللهِ لَا حَوْلَ وَلَا قُوَّةَ إِلَّا بِاللهِ. رَبَّنَا عَلَيْكَ تَوَكَّلْنَا وَإِلَيْكَ أَنَبْنَا وَإِلَيْكَ المَصِيرْ.

Ilāhī sukūtī kharasun yūjibu-ṣ-ṣamam, wa kalāmī ṣamamun yūjibu-l-bakam, wa-l-ḥayratu fī kulli dhālika wa lā ḥayrah. bismillāhi Rabbiya Allāh, bismillāhi Ḥasbiya Allāh, bismillāhi wa billāh, bismillāhi tawakkaltu ʿala-Allāh, bismillāhi saʾaltu mina-Allāh, bismillāhi lā ḥawla wa lā quwwata illā billāh. Rabbanā ʿalayka tawakkalnā wa ilayka anabnā wa ilayka-l-maṣīr.

Oh Allah, my silence is a muteness that necessitates deafness. My speech is a deafness that necessitates muteness. Indeed, perplexity is in all of this to no end. In the Name of Allah, my Lord is Allah, In the Name of Allah, Allah is Sufficient for me. In the Name of Allah and through Allah. In the Name of Allah, I rely upon Allah. In the Name of Allah, I ask from Allah. In the Name of Allah, there is no power nor strength save through Allah. Our Lord, upon You we depend, to You we repent and to You is the return.

اللهُمَّ إِنِّي أَسْأَلُكَ بِسِرِّ أَمْرِكَ وَعَظِيمِ قُدْرَتِكَ وَإِحَاطَةِ عِلْمِكَ وَخَصَائِصِ إِرَادَتِكَ وَتَأْثِيرِ قُدْرَتِكَ وَنُفُوذِ سَمْعِكَ وَبَصَرِكَ وَقَيُّومِيَّةِ حَيَاتِكْ، وَوُجُوبِ ذَاتِكَ وَصِفَاتِكْ، يَا اللهُ يَا اللهُ يَا اللهُ يَا أَوَّلُ يَا آخِرُ يَا ظَاهِرُ يَا بَاطِنْ، يَا نُورُ يَا حَيُّ يَا مُبِينْ.

Allāhumma innī asʾaluka bi-sirri amrika wa ʿaẓīmi qudratika wa iḥāṭati ʿilmika wa khaṣāʾiṣi irādatika wa taʾthīri qudratika wa nufūdhi samʿika wa baṣarika wa qayyūmiyyati ḥayātik, wa wujūbi dhātika wa ṣifātik, yā Allāhu yā Allāhu yā Allāhu yā Awwalu yā Ākhiru yā Ẓāhiru yā Bāṭin, yā Nūru yā Ḥayyu yā Mubīn.

Oh Allah, I ask You by the secret of Your Command, greatness of Your Power, envelopment of Your Knowledge, uniqueness of Your Will, effect of Your Power, omnipotence of Your Hearing and Sight, eternality of Your Life and Necessity of Your Essence and Attributes. Oh Allah, Oh Allah, Oh Allah, the First, Last, Outward, Inward, Light, All-Living, Most-Evident.

اللهُمَّ خَصِّصْ سِرِّي بِأَسْرَارِ وَحْدَانِيَّتِكْ، وَقَدِّسْ رُوحِي بِقُدْسِيَّةِ تَجَلِّيَاتِ صِفَاتِكْ، وَطَهِّرْ قَلْبِي بِطَهَارَةِ مَعَارِفِ إِلَهِيَّتِكْ. اللهُمَّ عَلِّمْ عَقْلِي مِنْ عُلُومِ لَدُنِّيَّتِكَ وَخَلِّقْ نَفْسِي بِأَخْلَاقِ رُبُوبِيَّتِكْ، وَأَيِّدْ حِسِّي بِمِدَادِ أَنْوَارِ حَضَرَاتِ نُورَانِيَّتِكْ، وَخَلِّصْ خُلَاصَةَ جَوَاهِرَ جُثْمَانِيَّتِي مِنْ قُيُودِ الطَّبْعِ وَكَثَافَةِ الحِسِّ وَحَصْرِ المَكَانِ وَالكَوْنْ.

Allāhumma khaṣṣiṣ sirrī bi-asrāri waḥdāniyyatik, wa qaddis rūḥī bi-qudsiyyati tajalliyāti ṣifātik, wa ṭahhir qalbī bi-ṭahārati maʿārifi ilāhiyyatik. wa ayyid ḥissī bi-midādi anwāri ḥaḍarāti nūrāniyyatik, wa khalliṣ khulāṣata jawāhira juthmāniyyatī min quyūdi-ṭ-ṭabʿi wa kathāfati-l-ḥissi wa ḥaṣri-l-makāni wa-l-kawn.

Oh Allah, elect my secret to be among those of Your Oneness, sanctify my spirit with the Sanctity of Your Attributes' Manifestations, purify my heart with the purity of the knowledges of Your Divinity. Oh Allah, teach my intellect from Your Knowledges, characterize my soul with the traits of Your Lordship, support my senses with a sustenance from the lights of the presences of Your Illumination, purify the quintessence of my form's core from the chains of habit, density of sense and constriction of place and universe.

اللهُمَّ وَانْقُلْنِي مِنْ دَرَكَاتِ خَلْقِي وَخُلُقِي إِلَى دَرَجَاتِ حَقِّكَ وَحَقِيقَتِكْ. أَنْتَ وَلِيِّ وَمَوْلَايَ وَبِكَ مَمَاتِي وَمَحْيَايَ إِيَّاكَ نَعْبُدُ وَإِيَّاكَ

نَسْتَعِينْ. انظُرْ اللهُمَّ إِلَيَّ نَظْرَةً تُنَظِّمُ بِهَا جَمِيعَ أَطْوَارِي وَتُطَهِّرُ بِهَا سِيرَةَ أَسْرَارِي، وَتَرْفَعُ بِهَا فِي المَلَأِ الأَعْلَى أَرْوَاحَ أَذْكَارِي وَتُقَوِّيَ بِهَا مِدَادَ أَنْوَارِي.

Allāhumma wa-nqulnī min darakāti khalqī wa khuluqī ilā darajāti ḥaqqika wa ḥaqīqatik. Anta Waliyyī wa Mawlāya wa bika mamātī wa maḥyāya Iyyāka naʿbudu wa Iyyāka nastaʿīn. unẓur Allāhumma ilayya naẓratan tunaẓẓimu bihā jamīʿa aṭwārī wa tuṭahhiru bihā sīrata asrārī, wa tarfaʿu bihā fi-l-malaʾi-l-aʿlā arwāḥa adhkārī wa tuqawwiya bihā midāda anwārī.

Oh Allah, move me from the depths of my mold and traits to the ranks of Your Truth and Reality. You are my Guardian and Protector, through You is my death and life, You do we worship and from You do we seek aid. Gaze upon me, oh Allah, with a gaze that rectifies all my states, purifies the journey of my secrets, elevates among the highest gathering the spirits of my remembrances and strengthens the sustenance of my lights.

اللهُمَّ غَيِّبْنِي عَنْ جَمِيعِ خَلْقِكَ وَاجْمَعْنِي عَلَيْكَ بِحَقِّكَ وَاحْفَظْنِي بِشُهُودِ تَصَرُّفَاتِ أَمْرِكَ فِي عَوَالِمِ فَرْقِكْ. اللهُمَّ بِكَ تَوَسَّلْتُ وَمِنْكَ سَأَلْتُ وَإِلَيْكَ تَوَجَّهْتُ وَفِيكَ لَا فِي شَيْءٍ سِوَاكَ رَغِبْتُ لَا أَسْأَلُ مِنْكَ سِوَاكَ وَلَا أَطْلُبُ مِنْكَ إِلَّا إِيَّاكْ.

Allāhumma ghayyibnī ʿan jamīʿi khalqika wa-jmaʿnī

ʿalayka bi-ḥaqqika wa-ḥfaẓnī bi-shuhūdi taṣarrufāti amrika fī ʿawālimi farqik. Allāhumma bika tawassaltu wa minka saʾaltu wa ilayka tawajjahtu wa fīka lā fī shayʾin siwāka raghibtu lā asʾalu minka siwāka wa lā aṭlubu minka illā Iyyāk.

Oh Allah, make me absent from all Your Creation, gather me upon You through Your Truth and guard me through witnessing the affairs of Your Command in the worlds of Your Separation. Oh Allah, through You I seek intercession, from You I ask, to You I have directed myself, in You and nothing else have I placed my desire. I ask naught from You save You, nor do I want from You save You.

اللهُمَّ وَأَتَوَسَّلُ إِلَيْكَ فِي قَبُولِ ذَلِكَ بِالوَسِيلَةِ العُظْمَى وَالفَضِيلَةِ الكُبْرَى وَالحَبِيبِ الأَدْنَى وَالوَلِيِّ المَوْلَى، مُحَمَّدٍ المُصْطَفَى وَالصَّفِيِّ المُرْتَضَى وَالنَّبِيِّ المُجْتَبَى، وَبِهِ أَسْأَلُكَ أَنْ تُصَلِّيَ عَلَيْهِ صَلَاةً أَبَدِيَّةً سَرْمَدِيَّةً أَزَلِيَّةً دَيْمُومِيَّةً إِلَهِيَّةً رَبَّانِيَّةً بِحَيْثُ تُشْهِدُنِي ذَلِكَ فِي عَيْنِ كَمَالِهِ وَتَسْتَهْلِكُنِي فِي شُهُودِ مَعَارِفِ ذَاتِه

Allāhumma wa atawassalu ilayka fī qabūli dhālika bi-l-wasīlati-l-ʿuẓmā wa-l-faḍīlati-l-kubrā wa-l-ḥabībi-l-adnā wa-l-waliyyi-l-mawlā, Muḥammadini-l-muṣṭafā wa-ṣ-ṣafiyyi-l-murtaḍā wa-n-nabiyyi-l-mujtabā, wa bihi asʾaluka an tuṣalliya ʿalayhi ṣalātan abadiyyatan sarmadiyyatan azaliyyatan daymūmiyyatan ilāhiyyatan rabbāniyyatan bi-ḥaythu tushhidunī dhālika fī ʿayni kamālihi wa tastahlikunī fī shuhūdi maʿārifi dhātih

Oh Allah, I also seek the intercession, for accepting this, of the greatest of means, largest bounty, nearest beloved and protected guardian, Muhammad ﷺ the chosen, content, purified companion, and elect prophet. And I ask You through him that You send upon him eternal, perpetual, pre-eternal, continuous, Divine and Lordly Prayers and to make me witness that in the essence of his perfection and consume me in witnessing the gnoses of his essence

وَعَلَى آلِهِ وَصَحْبِهِ كَذَلِكْ، فَإِنَّكَ وَلِيُّ ذَلِكَ وَلَا حَوْلَ وَلَا قُوَّةَ إِلَّا بِاللهِ
العَلِيِّ العَظِيمْ، وَالحَمْدُ للهِ رَبِّ العَالَمِينْ.

wa ʿalā ālihi wa ṣaḥbihi ka-dhālik, fa-innaka Waliyyu dhālika wa lā ḥawla wa lā quwwata illā billāhi-l-ʿAliyyi-l-ʿAẓīm, wa-l-ḥamdu lillāhi Rabbi-l-ʿālamīn.

And upon his family and companions likewise. Indeed, You are the custodian of this. There is no mean nor power save through Allah, the Most Lofty and Greatest. All praise is due to Allah the Lord of the worlds.

لَيْلَةُ الجُمُعَةِ

Laylatu-l-Jumuʿah

The Night of Friday

وَبِهِ نَسْتَعِينْ، إِلَهِي كُلُّ الأَبَاءُ العُلْوِيَّةُ عَبِيدُكَ وَأَنْتَ الرَّبُ عَلَى الإِطْلَاقْ. جَمَعْتَ بَيْنَ الْمُتَقَابِلَاتِ وَأَنْتَ الجَلِيلُ الجَمِيلُ لَا غَايَةَ لِابْتِهَاجِكَ بِذَاتِكَ إِذْ لَا غَايَةَ لِلشُّهُودِ مِنْك، أَنْتَ أَجَلُّ مِنْ شُهُودِنَا وَأَكْمَلُ وَأَعْلَى مِمَّا نَصِفُكَ بِهِ وَأَجْمَلْ، تَعَالَيْتَ فِي جَلَالِكَ عَنْ سِمَاتِ المُحْدَثَاتْ،

wa bihi nastaʿīn, Ilāhī kullu-l-ābāʾu-l-ʿulwuiyyatu ʿabīduka wa Anta-r-Rabbu ʿala-l-iṭlāq. jamaʿta bayna-l-mutaqābilāti wa Anta-l-Jalīlu-l-Jamīlu lā ghāyata li-btihājika bi-dhātika idh lā ghāyata li-sh-shuhūdi mink, Anta ajallu min shuhūdinā wa akmalu wa aʿlā mi-m-mā naṣifuka bihi wa ajmal, taʿālayta fī jalālika ʿan simāti-l-muḥdathāt,

And upon Him do we depend. Oh Allah, all higher fathers are Your Servants, while you are the Lord absolutely. You have gathered opposites; You are the Majestic and Beautiful. There is no end to Your Joyousness through Your Essence, for there is no end to witnessing from You, You are more Sublime than our witnessing and more Perfect and Loftier than what we ascribe to You, and more beautiful. You are Elevated in Your Majesty from the traits of incidents,

وَتَقَدَّسَ جَمَالُكَ العَلِيُّ عَنْ الْمُيُولِ إِلَيْهِ بِالشَّهَوَاتْ، أَسْأَلُكَ بِالسِّرِ الَّذِي جَمَعْتَ بِهِ بَيْنَ الْمُتَقَابِلَاتِ أَنْ تَجْمَعَ عَلَيَّ مُتَفَرَّقَ أَمْرِي جَمْعًا يُشْهِدُنِي وَحْدَةَ وُجُودِكْ، وَاكْسُنِي حُلَّةَ جَمَالِكْ، وَتَوِّجْنِي بِتَاجِ جَلَالِكَ حَتَّى تَخْضَعَ لِي النُّفُوسُ الْبَشَرِيَّةُ وَتَنْقَادَ إِلَيَّ الْقُلُوبُ الأَبِيَّةْ،

wa taqaddasa jamāluka-l-ʿaliyyu ʿani-l-muyūli ilayhi bi-sh-shahawāt, asʾaluka bi-s-sirri al-ladhī jamaʿta bihi bayna-l-mutaqābilāti an tajmaʿa ʿalayya mutafarraqa amrī jamʿan yushhidunī waḥdata wujūdik, wa-ksunī ḥullata jamālik, wa tawwijnī bi-tāji jalālika ḥattā takhḍaʿa li-n-nufūsu-l-bashiriyyatu wa tanqāda ilayya-l-qulūbu-l-abiyyah,

Your Lofty Beauty is sanctified from being an attraction to lowly desires. I ask You, by the secret through which You have gathered opposites, that You gather for me my dispersed affair, a gathering that allows me to witness the unity of Your Being. Dress me with the ornament of Your Beauty, and crown me with the embellishment of Your Majesty so that human souls submit to me, and stubborn hearts follow me,

وَتَنْبَسِطُ لَدَيَّ الأَسْرَارُ الأَقْدَسِيَّةْ، وَأَعْلِ قَدْرِي عِنْدَكَ عُلُوًّا يَنْخَفِضُ بِهِ كُلُّ مُتَعَالٍ وَيَذِلُّ لِي بِهِ كُلُّ عَزِيزْ وَخُذْ بِنَاصِيَتِي وَمَلِّكْنِي نَاصِيَةَ كُلِّ ذِي رُوحٍ نَاصِيَتُهُ بِيَدِكَ وَاجْعَلْ لِي لِسَانَ صِدْقٍ فِي خَلْقِكَ وَأَمْرِكْ، وَامْلَأْنِي مِنْكْ، وَاحْفَظْنِي فِي بَرِّكَ وَبَحْرِكْ، وَاَخْرِجْنِي مِنْ

قَرْيَةِ الطَّبْعِ الظَّالِمِ أَهْلُهَا،

wa tanbasiṭu ladayya-l-asrāru-l-aqdasiyyah, wa aʿli qadrī ʿindaka ʿuluwwan yankhafiḍu bihi kullu mutaʿālin wa yadhillu lī bihi kullu ʿazīz wa khudh bi-nāṣiyatī wa mallikni nāṣiyata kulli dhī rūḥin nāṣiyatuhu bi-yadika wa-jʿal lī lisāna ṣidqin fī khalqika wa amrik, wa-mlaʾnī mink, wa-ḥfaẓnī fī barrika wa baḥrik, wa akhrijnī min qariyati-ṭ-ṭabʿi-ẓ-ẓālimi ahluhā,

and the holiest secrets are spread forth before me. Elevate my worth with You such that every arrogant soul is lowered, and every difficult affair is made humble before me. Take me by the forelock and grant me ownership of the forelock of everyone with a spirit whose forelock is in Your Hand. Give me a tongue of truth among Your Creation and Command. Fill me of You, protect me in Your Land and Sea, and take me out from the abode of habits whose residents are unjust,

وَاعْتِقْنِي مِنْ رِقِّ الأَكْوَانْ، وَاجْعَلْ غِنَائِي فِي الفَقْرِ إِلَيْكَ عَنْ كُلِّ مَطْلُوبْ، وَاصْحَبْنِي بِعِنَايَتِكَ عَنْ كُلِّ مَرْغُوبْ. أَنْتَ وُجْهَتِي وَجَاهِي وَإِلَيْكَ المَرْجِعُ وَالتَّنَاهِي، تَجْبُرُ الكَسِيرَ وَتَكْسِرُ الجَبَّارِينَ وَتُجِيرُ الخَائِفِينَ وَتُخِيفُ الظَّالِمِينْ. لَكَ المَجْدُ الأَرْفَعُ وَالتَّجَلِي الأَجْمَعُ وَالحِجَابُ الأَمْنَعْ.

wa-ʿtiqnī min riqqi-l-akwān, wa-jʿal ghināʾī fi-l-faqri ilayka ʿan kulli maṭlūb, wa-ṣḥabnī bi-ʿināyatika ʿan kulli marghūb. Anta wujhāti wa jāhī wa ilayka-l-marjiʿu wa-t-tanāhī, tajbiru-l-kasīra wa taksiru-l-jabbārīna wa tujīru-l-khāʾifīna wa tukhīfa-ẓ-ẓālimīn. laka-l-majdu-l-arfaʿu wa-t-tajalli-l-ajmaʿu wa-l-ḥijābu-l-amnaʿ.

Liberate me from the servitude of universes and make my sufficiency in my need for You, away from every other desire. Accompany me with Your Care, away from every want. You are my direction and honor and to You is the return and the end. You mend the broken, break the arrogant, protect the fearful and frighten the unjust. To You belongs the loftiest nobility, all-encompassing manifestation, and most impenetrable veil.

سُبْحَانَكَ لَا إِلَهَ إِلَّا أَنْتَ أَنْتَ حَسْبِي وَنِعْمَ الوَكِيلُ. ﴿وَكَذَٰلِكَ أَخْذُ رَبِّكَ إِذَا أَخَذَ الْقُرَىٰ وَهِيَ ظَٰلِمَةٌ إِنَّ أَخْذَهُ أَلِيمٌ شَدِيدٌ﴾[53] ﴿فَانْتَقَمْنَا مِنَ الَّذِينَ أَجْرَمُوا وَكَانَ حَقًّا عَلَيْنَا نَصْرُ الْمُؤْمِنِينَ﴾[54] اللهُمَّ يَا خَالِقَ الْمَخْلُوقَاتِ وَيَا مُحْيِيَ الأَمْوَاتِ وَجَامِعَ الشَّتَاتِ وَمُفِيضَ الأَنْوَارِ عَلَى الذَّوَاتْ

subḥānaka lā ilāha illā Anta Anta ḥasbī wa niʿma-l-Wakīl. "Wa ka-dhālika akhdhu Rabbika idhā akhadha-l-qurā wa hiya ẓālimatun inna akhdhahu alīmun shadīd" "Fa-ntaqmnā mina-l-ladhīna ajramū wa kāna ḥaqqan ʿalaynā naṣru-l-muʾminīn" Allāhumma yā Khāliqa-l-makhlūqāti

---

53 هود 102

54 الروم 47

wa yā Muḥiyya-l-amwāti wa Jāmiʿa-sh-shatāti wa Mufiḍa-l-anwāri ʿala-dh-dhawāt

Glory be to You, there is no god but You. You are Sufficient for me and the best of supporters. "Like so is the seizing of Your Lord when He Seizes the towns while they are unjust. Indeed, His Seizing is painful and swift" "And so, We took revenge on those who transgressed, and it is binding from Us to assist the believers" Oh Allah, Creator of creation, Resurrector of the dead, Gatherer of scatters and Pourer of lights upon essences

لَكَ الْمُلْكُ الأَوْسَعُ وَالجَنَابُ الأَرْفَعُ، الأَرْبَابُ عَبِيدُكَ وَالْمُلُوكُ خَدَمَتُكْ، وَالأَغْنِيَاءُ فُقَرَاؤُكْ، وَأَنْتَ الغَنِيُّ بِذَاتِكَ عَمَّنْ سِوَاكْ. أَسْأَلُكَ بِإِسْمِكَ الَّذِي خَلَقْتَ بِهِ كُلَّ شَيْءٍ فَقَدَّرْتَهُ تَقْدِيرًا، وَمَنَحْتَ بِهِ مَنْ شِئْتَ جَنَّةً وَحَرِيرًا وَخِلَافَةً وَمُلْكًا كَبِيرًا، أَنْ تُذْهِبَ حِرْصِي وَتُكْمِلَ نَقْصِي

laka-l-mulku-l-awsaʿu wa-l-janābu-l-arfaʿ, al-arbābu ʿabīduka wa-l-mulūku khadamatuk, wa-l-aghniyāʾu fuqarāʾuk, wa Anta-l-Ghaniyyu bi-dhātika ʿamman siwāk. asʾaluka bi-ismika al-ladhī khalaqta bihi kulla shayʾin fa-qaddartahu taqdīra, wa manaḥta bihi man shiʾta jannatan wa ḥarīran wa khilāfatan wa mulkan kabīra, an tudhhiba ḥirṣī wa tukmila naqṣī

To You belongs the most expansive dominion and loftiest honor. All lords are Your Slaves, kings Your Servants and the rich are Your Poor, while You are the Sufficient One through Your Essence, not in need of anyone else. I ask You by Your Name through which You have created everything and decreed its measure, granted whomever You Will a silken paradise, deputyship, and large dominion, that You remove my greed and mend my shortcomings

وَأَنْ تُفِيضَ عَلَيَّ مِنْ مَلَابِسَ نَعَمَائِكَ وَتُعَلِّمَنِي مِنْ أَسْمَائِكَ مَا يَصْلُحُ لِلأَذَى وَالإِيلَافْ، وَامْلَأْ بَاطِنِي خَشْيَةً وَرَحْمَةً وَظَاهِرِي هَيْبَةً وَعَظَمَةً حَتَّى تَخَافَنِي قُلُوبُ الأَعْدَاءِ وَتَرْتَاحَ إِلَيَّ أَرْوَاحُ الأَوْلِيَاءِ ﴿يَخَافُونَ رَبَّهُمْ مِنْ فَوْقِهِمْ وَيَفْعَلُونَ مَا يُؤْمَرُونَ﴾[55]

wa an tufiḍa ʿalayya min malābisa naʿamāʾika wa tuʿallimanī min asmāʾika mā yāṣluḥu li-l-adhā wa-l-īlāf, wa-mlaʾ bāṭinī khashiyatan wa raḥmatan wa ẓāhirī haybatan wa ʿaẓamatan ḥattā takhāfanī qulūbu-l-aʿdāʾi wa tartāḥa ilayya arwāḥu-l-awliyāʾ "Yakhāfūna Rabbahum min fawqihim wa yafʿalūna mā yuʾmarūn"

And that You pour upon me from the garments of Your Bounties and teach me of Your Names what befits both, harm, and harmony. Fill my inward with awareness and mercy and my outward of awe and greatness so that the hearts of enemies fear me, and spirits of saints find tranquility in me. "They fear their Lord above them and fulfill what they are commanded"

---

[55] النحل 50

رَبِّ هَيِّءْ لِي سَعَادَةً كَامِلَةً لِقَبُولِ فَيْضِكَ الأَقْدَسَ لِأَخْلُفَكَ فِي بِلَادِكَ وَارْفَعَ بِهِ سَخَطَكَ عَنْ عِبَادِكْ. تَسْتَخْلِفُ مَنْ تَشَاءُ وَأَنْتَ عَلَى كُلِّ شَيْءٍ قَدِيرْ، وَأَنْتَ الخَبِيرُ البَصِيرُ وَصَلَّى اللهُ عَلَى سَيِّدِنَا مُحَمَّدٍ وَآلِهِ وَصَحْبِهِ وَسَلَّمَ وَهُوَ حَسْبِي وَنِعْمَ الوَكِيلْ.

Rabbi hayyiʾ lī saʿādatan kāmilatan li-qabūli fayḍika-l-aqdasa li-akhlufaka fī bilādika wa arfaʿa bihi sakhaṭaka ʿan ʿibādik. tastakhlifu man tashāʾu wa Anta ʿalā kulli shayʾin Qadīr, wa Anta-l-Khabīru-l-Baṣīru wa ṣallā Allāhu ʿalā sayyidinā Muḥammadin wa ālihi wa ṣaḥbihi wa sallama wa Huwa ḥasbī wa niʿma-l-Wakīl.

Oh, my Lord, prepare for me a perfect happiness to accept Your Holiest Emanation, to be Your Deputy in Your Lands and lift, through it, Your Anger from upon Your Servants. You entrust whomever You Will, and You are All Able to do everything. You are the All-Aware and All-Seeing. May Allah send His Prayers upon our master Muhammad ﷺ, his family and companions with abundant salutations. Indeed, He is sufficient for me and the best of supporters.

يَوْمُ الجُمُعَةِ

Yawmu-l-Jumuʿah

The Day of Friday

رَبِّ رَقِّنِي فِي مَدَارِجِ المَعَارِفْ، وَقَلِّبْنِي فِي أَطْوَارِ أَسْرَارِ الحَقَائِقِ وَاحْجُبْنِي فِي سُرَادِقَاتِ حِفْظِكَ وَمَكْنُونِ سِرِّ سَتْرِكَ عَنْ وُرُودِ الخَوَاطِرِ الَّتِي لَا تَلِيقُ بِسُبُحَاتِ جَلَالِكْ، رَبِّ أَقِمْنِي بِكَ فِي كُلِّ شَأْنْ، وَأَشْهِدْنِي لُطْفَكَ فِي كُلِّ قَاصٍ وَدَانْ،

Rabbi raqqinī fī madāriji-l-maʿārif, wa qallibnī fī aṭwāri asrāri-l-ḥaqāʾiqi wa-ḥjubnī fī surādiqāti ḥifẓika wa maknūni sirri satrika ʿan wurūdi-l-khawāṭiri al-latī lā talīqu bi-subuḥāti jalālik, Rabbi aqimnī bika fī kulli shaʾn, wa ashhidnī luṭfaka fī kulli qāṣin wa dān,

Oh Allah, ascend me in the ranks of gnoses, fluctuate me in the stage of the secrets of reality and veil me, within the treasuries of Your Protection and shelter of the secret of Your Envelopment, from the arrival of thoughts that do not befit the glories of Your Majesty. Oh, my Lord, establish me through You in every affair, and grant me to witness Your Clemency in all that is distant and near,

وَافْتَحْ عَيْنَ بَصِيرَتِي فِي فَضَاءِ سَاحَةِ التَّوْحِيدِ لِأَشْهَدَ قِيَامَ الكُلِّ بِكَ شُهُودًا يَقْطَعُ نَظَرِي عَنْ كُلِّ مَوْجُودٍ يَا ذَا الفَضْلِ وَالجُودْ. رَبِّ أَفِضْ عَلَيَّ مِنْ بِحَارِ تَجْرِيدِ أَلِفِ الذَّاتِ الأَقْدَسِ

مَا يَقْطَعُ عَنِّي كُلَّ عِلَاقَةٍ تَعْجُمُ إِدْرَاكِي وَتُغْلِقُ دُونِي بَابَ مَطْلَبِي،

wa-ftaḥ ʿayna baṣīratī fī faḍāʾi sāḥati-t-tawḥīdi li-ashhada qiyāma-l-kulli bika shuhūdan yaqṭaʿu naẓarī ʿan kulli mawjūdin yā Dha-l-Faḍli wa-l-Jūd. Rabbi afiḍ ʿalayya min biḥāri tajrīdi alifi-dh-dhāti-l-aqdasi mā yaqṭaʿu ʿannī kulla ʿilāqatin taʿjumu idrākī wa tughliqu dūnī bāba maṭlabī,

Open the eye of my insight in the expanse of the courtyard of monotheism so that I may witness the rising of all through You, a witnessing that cuts my gaze away from every existent thing, oh One of Bounty and Generosity. Oh, my Lord, overflow upon me from the seas of the transcendent Alif of the Holiest Essence, such that it cuts from me every relationship that hinders my comprehension and closes the door of my desire,

وَاسْبُلْ عَلَيَّ مِنْ هَيُولِي نُقْطَتِهَا الكُلِّيَّةِ البَارِزَةِ مِنْ مَلَكُوتِ غَيْبِ ذَاتِكَ مَا أَمُدُّ بِهِ حُرُوفَ الأَكْوَانْ، وَاجْعَلْنِي مَحْفُوظًا فِي ذَاتِكَ مِنْ النَّقْصِ وَالشَّيْنْ. يَا مَنْ وَسِعَ كُلَّ شَيْءٍ رَحْمَةً وَعِلْمًا يَا رَبَّ العَالَمِينْ. رَبِّ طَهِّرْنِي ظَاهِرًا وَبَاطِنًا مِنْ لَوْثِ الأَغْيَارِ وَالوُقُوفِ عَلَى الأَطْوَارِ بِقَبْضٍ مِنْ ظُهُورِ نُورِ قُدْسِكْ

wa-sbul ʿalayya min hayūlī nuqṭatiha-l-kulliyyati-l-bārizati min malakūti ghaybi dhātika mā amuddu bihi ḥurūfa-l-akwān, wa-jʿalnī maḥfūẓan fī dhātika mina-n-naqṣi wa-sh-shayn. yā man wasiʿa kulla shayʾin raḥmatan wa ʿilman yā Rabbi-l-ʿālamīn. Rabbi ṭahhirnī ẓāhiran wa bāṭinan min lawthi-l-aghiyāri wa-l-wuqūfi ʿala-l-aṭwāri bi-qabḍin min ẓuhūri nūri qudsik

And unfurl upon me from the matter of its all-encompassing dot that emerges from the dominion of the unseen of Your Essence with what I may sustain, through it, of the letters of the universe. Make me preserved in Your Essence from shortcomings and blame. Oh, You who has encompassed everything in Mercy and Knowledge oh Lord of the worlds. My Lord, purify me outwardly and inwardly from the filth of othering[56] and halting at mediations through a constriction from Your Manifesting Light of Holiness.

وَغَيِّبْنِي عَنْهُمْ بِشُهُودِ بَوَارِقِ أُنْسِكْ، وَاطْلِعْنِي عَلَى حَقَائِقِ الأَشْيَاءِ وَدَقَائِقِ الأَشْكَالْ، وَاسْمِعْنِي نُطْقَ الأَكْوَانِ بِصَرِيحِ تَوْحِيدِكَ فِي العَوَالِمِ كُلِّهَا وَقَابِلْ مِرْآتِي بِتَجَلٍّ تَامٍّ مِنْ جَوَاهِرِ أَسْمَاءِ جَلَالِكَ وَقَهْرِكْ، فَلَا يَقَعُ عَلَيَّ بَصَرُ جَبَّارٍ مِنْ الإِنْسِ وَالجِنِّ إِلَّا انْعَكَسَ عَلَيْهِ مِنْ شُعَاعِ ذَلِكَ الجَوْهَرِ

wa ghayyibnī ʿanhum bi-shuhūdi bawāriqi unsik, wa aṭliʿnī ʿalā ḥaqāʾiqi-l-ashiyāʾi wa daqāʾiqi-l-ashkāl, wa asmiʿnī nuṭqa-l-akwāni bi-ṣarīḥi tawḥīdika fi-l-ʿawālimi kullihā wa qābil mirʾātī bi-tajallin tāmmin min jawāhiri asmāʾi jalālika wa qahrik, fa-lā yaqaʿu ʿalayya baṣaru jabbārin mina-l-insi wa-l-jinni illa-nʿakasa ʿalayhi min shuʿāʿi dhālika-l-jawhari

---

56 The 'filth of othering' is a lowly state where the seeker is distracted from Allah by anything other than Him.

Make me absent from them by witnessing glimpses of Your Intimacy. Show me the realities of things and details of forms. Let me hear the universes clearly declaring Your Oneness in all the worlds. Meet my mirror with a complete manifestation from the essences of Your Names of Majesty and Subduing, such that no gaze of any tyrant, human or jinn, falls upon me save that a ray from that essence returns to them

مَا تَحْرِقُ نَفْسَهُ الأَمَّارَةَ بِالسُّوءِ وَتَرُدَّهُ ضَالًّا ذَلِيلًا وَيَنْقَلِبُ عَنِّي بَصَرُهُ خَاسِئًا كَلِيلًا. يَا مَنْ عَنَتْ لَهُ الوُجُوهُ وَخَضَعَتْ لَهُ الرِّقَابُ يَا رَبَّ الأَرْبَابْ. رَبِّ أَبْعِدْنِي عَنْ القَوَاطِعِ الَّتِي تَقْطَعُنِي عَنْ حَضَرَاتِ قُدْسِكْ، وَاسْلُبْنِي مَا لَا يَلِيقُ مِنْ صِفَاتِي بِغَلَبَةِ أَنْوَارِ صِفَاتِكْ،

mā taḥriqu nafsahu-l-ammāratu bi-s-sū'i wa taruddahu ḍāllan dhalīlan wa yanqalibu ʿannī baṣarahu khāsi'an kalīla. yā man ʿanat lahu-l-wujūhu wa khaḍaʿat lahu-r-riqābu yā Rabba-l-arbāb. Rabbi abʿidnī ʿani-l-qawāṭiʿi al-latī taqṭaʿunī ʿan ḥaḍarāti qudsik, wa-slubnī mā lā yalīqu min ṣifātī bi-ghalabati anwāri ṣifātik,

and burns their ego that commands evil, sending them back astray and humiliated and their gaze is turned away from me lost and weakened. Oh, You to whom faces are humbled and necks are lowered, oh Lord of lords. My Lord, keep me away from those deterrents that cut me from the presences of Your Holiness. Deprive me of those traits that are not befitting the overwhelming lights of Your Attributes,

وَأَزِحْ ظُلْمَ طَبْعِي وَبَشَرِيَّتِي بِتَجَلِّ بَارِقٍ مِنْ بَوَارِقِ نُورِ ذَاتِكْ،
وَامْدُدْنِي بِقُوَّةٍ مَلَكِيَّةٍ أَقْهَرُ بِهَا مَا اسْتَوْلَى عَلَيَّ مِنَ الطَّبَائِعِ الدَّنِيَّةِ
وَالأَخْلَاقِ الرَّدِيَّةِ وَامْحُ مِنْ لَوْحِ فِكْرِي أَشْكَالَ الأَكْوَانِ وَاثْبُتْ فِيهِ
بِيَدِ عِنَايَتِكَ سِرِّ حِرْزِ قُرْبِكَ السَّابِقِ المَكْنُونِ بَيْنَ الكَافِ وَالنُّونْ

wa aziḥ ẓulma ṭabʿī wa bashariyyatī bi-tajalli bāriqin min bawāriqi nūri dhātik, wa-mdudnī bi-quwwatin malakiyyatin aqharu bihā ma-stawlā ʿalayya mina-ṭ-ṭabāyiʿi-d-daniyyati wa-l-akhlāqi-r-radiyyati wa-mḥu min lawḥi fikrī ashkāla-l-akwāni wa-thbut fīhi bi-yadi ʿināyatika sirri ḥirzi qurbika-s-sābiqi-l-maknūni bayna-l-kāfi wa-n-nūn

Remove the darkness of my mold and humanness through a manifestation of a flash from those of the Light of Your Essence. Sustain me with an angelic power through which I may subdue what has overcome me of lowly habits and filthy traits. Erase from the tablet of my reflection the forms of universes and make firm therein, with the hand of Your Care, the secret share of Your Nearness that is preordained and hidden between Kāf and Nūn[57]

يَا نُورَ النُّورِ يَا مُفِيضَ الكُلِّ مِنْ فَيْضِهِ المِدْرَارْ، يَا قُدُّوسُ يَا صَمَدُ يَا
حَفِيظُ يَا لَطِيفُ يَا رَبَّ العَالَمِينْ،

---

[57] The reference here is to the و (waw) in *Kun* (Be) which is the Divine Command for creation to take place.

وَصَلَّى اللهُ عَلَى سَيِّدِنَا مُحَمَّدٍ وَآلِهِ وَصَحْبِهِ أَجْمَعِينْ، وَالحَمْدُ للهِ رَبِّ العَالَمِينْ.

yā Nūra-n-nūri yā Mufiḍa-l-kulli min fayḍihi-l-midrār, yā Quddūsu yā Ṣamadu yā Ḥafiẓu yā Laṭīfu yā Rabba-l-ʿālamīn, wa ṣallā Allāhu ʿalā sayyidinā Muḥammadin wa ālihi wa ṣaḥbihi ajmaʿīn, wa-l-ḥamdu lillāhi Rabbi-l-ʿālamīn.

Oh, Light of light, Inundator of everyone from His Overflowing Flood. Oh Most-Holy, Self-Sufficient, Guardian, Most-Subtle and Most-Gentle Lord of the worlds. May Allah send His Prayers upon our master Muhammad ﷺ, his family and companions entirely. All praise is due to Allah, the Lord of the worlds.

لَيْلَةُ السَّبْتْ

Laylatu-s-Sabt

The Night of Saturday

سَيِّدِي دَامَ بَقَاؤُكَ وَنَفَذَ فِي الخَلْقِ قَضَاؤُكَ وَتَقَدَّسْتَ فِي عُلُوِّكَ وَتَعَالَيْتَ فِي قُدْسِكْ. لَا يَؤُدُكَ حِفْظُ كَوْنٍ وَلَا يَخْفَى عَنْكَ كَشْفُ عَيْنْ. تَدْعُو مَنْ تَشَاءُ إِلَيْكَ وَتَدُلُّ بِكَ عَلَيْكْ، فَلَكَ الحَمْدُ الدَّائِمُ وَالدَّوَامُ الأَمْجَدْ. أَسْأَلُكَ وَقْتًا صَافِيًا بِمَا تُرِيدُ بِمُعَامَلَةٍ لَائِقَةٍ تَكُونُ غَايَتُهَا قُرْبُكَ مِنْ نَتَائِجِ الأَعْمَالِ

Sayyidī dāma baqāʾuka wa nafadha fi-l-khalqi qaḍāʾuka wa taqaddasta fī ʿuluwwika wa taʿālayta fī qudsik. lā yaʾūduka ḥifẓu kawnin wa lā yakhfā ʿanka kashfu ʿayn. tadʿū man tashāʾu ilayka wa tadullu bika ʿalayk, fa-laka-l-ḥamdu-l-dāʾimu wa-d-dawāmu-l-amjad. asʾaluka waqtan ṣāfiyan bi-mā turīdu bi-muʿāmalatin lāʾiqatin takūnu ghāyatuhā qurbuka min natāʾiji-l-aʿmāli

Oh, my Master, Your Subsistence has persisted and Your Judgment in creation is fulfilled. You are sanctified in Your Loftiness and lofty in Your Holiness. You are not burdened by the guarding of a universe, nor is the unveiling of any essence hidden from You. You call whomever You will to You and guide, through You, to You. Thus, to You belongs the continuous praise and noble continuity. I ask You a pure moment, as You decree, with a befitting treatment, the destination of which is Your Nearness at the ends of deeds

مَوْقُوفَةٌ عَلَى رِضْوَانِكْ، وَهَبْ لِي سِرًّا زَاهِرًا يَكْشِفُ لِي عَنْ حَقَائِقِ الأَعْمَالْ، وَاخْصُصْنِي بِحِكْمَةٍ مَعَهَا حُكْمٌ، وَإِشَارَةٍ يَصْحَبُهَا فَهْمْ. إِنَّكَ وَلِيُّ مَنْ تَوَلَّاكَ وَتُجِيبُ مَنْ دَعَاكْ. إِلَهِي أَدِمْ بَقَاءَ نَعَمَائِكَ عَلَيَّ وَمُشَاهَدَتِكَ لَدَيَّ وَأَشْهِدْنِي ذَاتِي مِنْ حَيْثُ أَنْتَ لَا مِنْ حَيْثُ هِيَ حَتَّى أَكُونَ بِكَ وَلَا أَنَا.

mawqūfatun ʿalā riḍwānik, wa hab lī sirran zāhiran yakshifu lī ʿan ḥaqāʾiqi-l-aʿmāl, wa-khṣuṣnī bi-ḥikmatin maʿahā ḥukmun, wa ishāratin yaṣḥabuhā fahm. Innaka Waliyyu man tawallāka wa tujību man daʿāk. Ilāhī adim baqāʾa naʿamāʾika ʿalayya wa mushāhadatika ladayya wa ashhidnī dhātī min ḥaythu Anta lā min ḥaythu hiya ḥattā akūna bika wa lā anā.

Halting at Your Contentment. Gift me a splendid secret that unveils for me the realities of deeds. Distinguish me by a wisdom alongside a ruling and an allusion accompanied by comprehension. Indeed, You are the Guardian of he who takes You as a Guardian and the Responder to he who supplicates to You. Oh Allah, maintain for me the subsistence of Your Bounties and witnessing You. Grant me to witness my essence as You Are, not as it is, so that I may be through You, not myself.

وَهَبْ لِي مِنْ لَدُنْكَ عِلْمًا تَنْقَادُ إِلَيَّ فِيهِ كُلُّ رُوحٍ عَالِمَةٍ إِنَّكَ أَنْتَ

العَلِيمُ العَلَّامُ ﴿تَبَـٰرَكَ اسْمُ رَبِّكَ ذِي الجَلَـٰلِ وَالإِكْرَامِ﴾[58] ﴿وَعِنْدَهُ مَفَاتِحُ الغَيْبِ لَا يَعْلَمُهَا إِلَّا هُوَ وَيَعْلَمُ مَا فِي البَرِّ وَالبَحْرِ﴾[59] رَبِّ أَفِضْ عَلَيَّ شُعَاعًا مِنْ نُورِكَ يَكْشِفُ لِي عَنْ كُلِّ مَسْتُورٍ فِيَّ حَتَّى أُشَاهِدَ وُجُودِي كَامِلًا مِنْ حَيْثُ أَنْتَ لَا مِنْ حَيْثُ أَنَا

wa hab lī min ladunka ʿilman tanqādu ilayya fīhi kullu rūḥin ʿālimatin Innaka Anta-l-ʿAlīmu-l-ʿAllāmu "Tabāraka Ismu Rabbika Dhi-l-Jalāli wa-l-Ikrām" "Wa ʿIndahu mafātiḥu-l-ghaybi lā yaʿlamuhā illā Huwa wa yaʿlamu mā fi-l-barri wa-l-baḥr" Rabbi afiḍ ʿalayya shuʿāʿan min nūrika yakshifu lī ʿan kulli mastūrin fiyya ḥattā ushāhida wujūdī kāmilan min ḥaythu Anta lā min ḥaythu anā

Gift me from Yourself knowledge through which every knowledgeable spirit may follow me. Indeed, You are the All-Knower and All-Knowing "May the Name of Your Lord be blessed, He of Majesty and Generosity" "With Him are the keys of the unseen, none knows them but He. And He knows whatever is on the land and sea" Oh my Lord, overflow upon me a ray from Your Light that unveils for me every curtained thing within me, so that I may witness my being, perfected through You, not through me

---

58 الرحمن 78

59 الأنعام 56

فَأَتَقَرَّبَ إِلَيْكَ بِمَحْوِ صِفَتِي مِنِّي كَمَا تَقَرَّبْتَ إِلَيَّ بِإِضَافَةِ نُورِكَ عَلَيَّ. رَبِّ الإِمْكَانُ صِفَتِي وَالعَدَمُ مَادَّتِي وَالفَقْرُ قُوَّتِي وَوُجُودُكَ عِلَّتِي وَقُدْرَتُكَ فَاعِلِي وَأَنْتَ غَايَتِي. حَسْبِي مِنْكَ عِلْمُكَ بِجَهْلِي. أَنْتَ كَمَا أَعْلَمُ وَفَوْقَ مَا أَعْلَمُ وَأَنْتَ مَعَ كُلِّ شَيْءٍ وَلَيْسَ مَعَكَ شَيْءٌ.

fa-ataqarraba ilayka bi-maḥwi ṣifatī minnī ka-mā taqarrabta ilayya bi-iḍāfati nūrika ʿalayy. Rabbi-l-imkānu ṣifatī wa-l-ʿadamu māddatī wa-l-faqru quwwatī wa wujūduka ʿillatī wa qudratuka fāʿilī wa Anta ghāyatī. ḥasbī minka ʿilmuka bi-jahlī. Anta ka-mā aʿlamu wa fawqa mā aʿlamu wa Anta maʿa kulli shayʾin wa laysa maʿaka shayʾ.

So that I can draw nearer to You by effacing my attributes from me, just as You have drawn near to me by overflowing Your Light upon me. Oh, my Lord, contingency is my attribute, non-existence my mold, poverty my strength, Your Being my cause, Your Power my energy and You are my destination. Your Knowledge of my ignorance suffices me. You are as I know and above what I know, and You are with everything while nothing is with You.

قَدَّرْتَ المَنَازِلَ لِلسَّيْرِ وَرَتَّبْتَ المَرَاتِبَ لِلنَّفْعِ وَالضَّيْرِ، وَأَثْبَتَّ مِنْهَاجَ الخَيْرِ، فَنَحْنُ ذَلِكَ كُلُّهُ بِكَ وَأَنْتَ بِلَا نَحْنُ. فَأَنْتَ الخَيْرُ المَحْضُ وَالجُودُ الصِّرْفُ وَالكَمَالُ المُطْلَقُ.

أَسْأَلُكَ بِاسْمِكَ الَّذِي أَفَضْتَ بِهِ النُّورَ عَلَى القَوَابِلِ وَمَحَوْتَ بِهِ ظُلْمَةَ الغَوَاسِقِ أَنْ تَمْلأَ وُجُودِي نُورًا مِنْ نُورِكَ

qaddarta-l-manāzila li-s-sayr wa rattabta-l-marātiba li-n-naf'i wa-ḍ-ḍayr, wa athbatta minhāja-l-khayr, fa-naḥnu dhālika kulluhu bika wa Anta bi-lā naḥn. fa-Anta-l-Khayru-l-Maḥḍu wa-l-Jūdu-ṣ-Ṣirfu wa-l-Kamālu-l-Muṭlaq. as'aluka bi-ismika al-ladhī afaḍta bihi-n-nūra 'ala-l-qawābili wa maḥawta bihi ẓulmata-l-ghawāsiqi an tamla'a wujūdī nūran min nūrika

You measured the abodes for journeying, organized the ranks for benefit and harm and established the way to goodness. We are, in all of this, through You, while You are not through us. Indeed, You are the Essence of Goodness, Pure Generosity and Absolute Perfection. I ask You by Your Name through which You have overflowed lights upon the forms and erased the darkness of nights, that You fill my being with a light from Your Light

الَّذِي هُوَ مَادَّةُ كُلِّ نُورٍ وَغَايَةُ كُلِّ مَطْلُوبٍ، حَتَّى لَا يَخْفَى عَلَيَّ شَيْءٌ مِمَّا أَوْدَعْتَ فِي ذَرَّاتِ وُجُودِي، وَهَبْ لِي لِسَانَ صِدْقٍ مُعَبِّرًا عَنْ شُهُودِ حَقٍّ وَاخْصُصْنِي مِنْ جَوَامِعِ الكَلِمِ مَا يَحْصُلُ بِهِ الإِنَابَةُ وَالبَلَاغَةُ وَاعْصِمْنِي فِي كُلِّ كَلِمَةٍ مِنْ دَعْوَى مَا لَيْسَ لِي بِحَقْ

al-ladhī huwa māddatu kulli nūrin wa ghāyatu kulli maṭlūb, ḥattā lā yakhfā 'alayya shay'un mimmā awda'ta fī dharrāti wujūdī, wa hab lī lisāna ṣidqin mu'abbiran 'an shuhūdi ḥaqqin wa-khṣuṣnī min jawāmiʿi-l-kalimi mā yaḥṣulu bihi-l-inābatu wa-l-balāghatu wa-ʿṣimnī fī kulli kalimatin min daʿwā mā laysa lī bi-ḥaqq

Which is the matter of every light and goal of every desire, so that nothing that You have put in the atoms of my being is hidden from me. Gift me a tongue of truthfulness that expresses a witnessing of truth. Distinguish me with something from the all-encompassing speech to produce deputyship and conveyance. Guard me, in every word, from claiming what is not rightfully mine.

وَاجْعَلْنِي عَلَى بَصِيرَةٍ مِنْكَ أَنَا وَمَنْ اتَّبَعَنِي. اللهُمَّ إِنِّي أَعُوذُ بِكَ مِنْ قَوْلٍ يُوجِبُ حَيْرَةً أَوْ يُعْقِبُ فِتْنَةً أَوْ يُوهِمُ شُبْهَةً. مِنْكَ تُعْقَلُ الكَلِمُ وَعَنْكَ تُؤْخَذُ الحِكَمْ. أَنْتَ مُمْسِكُ السَّماءَ وَمُعَلِّمُ الأَسْمَاءْ، لَا إِلَهَ إِلَّا أَنْتَ الوَاحِدُ الأَحَدُ الفَرْدُ الصَّمَدُ الَّذِي لَمْ يَلِدْ وَلَمْ يُولَدْ وَلَمْ يَكُنْ لَهُ كُفُوًا أَحَدْ

wa-jʿalnī ʿalā baṣīratin minka anā wa mani-t-tabaʿanī. Allāhumma innī aʿūdhu bika min qawlin yūjibu ḥayratan aw yuʿqibu fitnatan aw yūhimu shubhah. minka tuʿqalu-l-kalimu wa ʿanka tuʾkhadhu-l-ḥikam. Anta mumsiku-s-samāʾa wa muʿallimu-l-asmāʾ, lā ilāha illā Anta-l-Wāḥidu-l-Aḥadu-l-Fardu-ṣ-Ṣamadu al-ladhī lam yalid wa lam yūlad wa lam yakun lahu kufuwan aḥad

Make me, and those who follow me, be upon an insight from You. Oh Allah, I seek refuge in You from a statement that mandates a perplexity, leaves behind a tribulation or illudes doubt. From You are words understood and wisdoms received. You are the Holder of heaven and Teacher of names. There is no god but You, the One, Singular, Unique, Self-Sufficient who neither begets children, is begotten nor has any equal.

وَصَلَّى اللهُ عَلَى سَيِّدِنَا مُحَمَّدٍ وَآلِهِ وَصَحْبِهِ أَجْمَعِينَ. سُبْحَـٰنَ رَبِّكَ رَبِّ الْعِزَّةِ عَمَّا يَصِفُونَ وَسَلَـٰمٌ عَلَى الْمُرْسَلِينَ وَالْحَمْدُ لله رَبِّ الْعَـٰلَمِينَ

wa ṣalla Allāhu ʿalā sayyidinā Muḥammadin wa ālihi wa ṣaḥbihi ajmaʿīn. Subḥāna Rabbika Rabbi-l-ʿIzzati ʿammā yaṣifūna wa salāmun ʿala-l-mursalīna wa-l-ḥamdu lillāhi Rabbi-l-ʿālamīn

May Allah send His Prayers upon our master Muhammad ﷺ, his family and companions entirely. Glory be to Your Lord, the Lord of Exaltedness above what they ascribe, and abundant salutations be upon the messengers. All praise is due to Allah, the Lord of the worlds.

يَوْمُ السَّبْتْ

Yawmu-s-Sabt

The Day of Saturday

وَمَنْ يَعْتَصِمْ بِالله فَقَدْ هُدِيَ إِلَى صِرَاطٍ مُسْتَقِيمْ، الحَمْدُ لله الَّذِي أَحَلَّنِي حِمَى لُطْفِ الله، الحَمْدُ لله الَّذِي أَنْزَلَنِي جَنَّةَ رَحْمَةِ الله، الحَمْدُ لله الَّذِي أَجْلَسَنِي فِي مَقَامِ مَحَبَّةِ الله، الحَمْدُ لله الَّذِي أَذَاقَنِي مِنْ مَوَائِدِ مَدَدِ الله، الحَمْدُ لله الَّذِي وَهَبَنِي لَطَافَةِ الإِضَافَةِ لِاصْطِفَاءِ الله،

wa man yaʿtaṣimu billāhi fa-qad hudiya ilā ṣirātin mustaqīm, al-ḥamdu lillāhi al-ladhī aḥallanī ḥimā luṭfi Allāh, al-ḥamdu lillāhi al-ladhī anzalanī jannata raḥmati Allāh, al-ḥamdu lillāhi al-ladhī ajlasanī fī maqāmi maḥabbati Allāh, al-ḥamdu lillāhi al-ladhī adhāqanī min mawāʾidi madadi Allāh, al-ḥamdu lillāhi al-ladhī wahabani laṭāfati-l-iḍāfati li-ṣṭifāʾi Allāh,

Whoever holds on to Allah has been guided to a straight path. All praise is due to Allah who settled me in the fortress of Allah's Gentleness. All praise is due to Allah who hosted me in the paradise of Allah's Mercy. All praise is due to Allah who seated me in the station of Allah's love. All praise is due to Allah who let me taste from the feasts of Allah's providence. All praise is due to Allah who gifted me the subtlety of being included in Allah's election.

الحَمْدُ لله الَّذِي سَقَانِي مِنْ مَوَارِدِ وَارِدِ وَفَاءِ الله، الحَمْدُ لله الَّذِي كَسَانِي حُلَلَ صِدْقِ العُبُودِيَّةِ لله، كُلُّ ذَلِكَ عَلَى مَا فَرَّطْتُ فِي جَنْبِ

اللهِ وَضَيَّعْتُ مِنْ حُقُوقِ اللهِ فَذَلِكَ الفَضْلُ مِنْ اللهِ وَمَنْ يَغْفِرُ الذُّنُوبَ إِلَّا اللهُ؟ إِلَهِي إِنْعَامُكَ عَلَيَّ بِالإِيجَادِ مِنْ غَيْرِ جُهْدٍ مِنِّي وَلَا اجْتِهَادْ.

al-ḥamdu lillāhi al-ladhī saqānī min mawāridi wāridi wafā῾i Allāh, al-ḥamdu lillāhi al-ladhī kasānī ḥulala ṣidqi-l-῾ubūdiyyati lillāh, kullu dhālika ῾alā mā farraṭtu fī janbi Allāh wa ḍayya῾tu min ḥuqūqi Allāh fa-dhālika-l-faḍlu min Allāh wa man yaghfiru-dh-dhunūba illa Allāh? Ilāhi in῾āmuka ῾alayya bi-l-ījādi min ghayr juhdin minni wa la-jtihād.

All praise is due to Allah who gave me to drink from the springs of fulfillments, arriving from Allah. All praise is due to Allah who clothed me from the ornaments of true servanthood to Allah. All of this despite what I have transgressed in the boundaries of Allah and overlooked of the rights of Allah. That is the bounty from Allah, and who forgives sins but Allah? Oh Allah, Your Bestowal upon me with generosity is without any struggle on my part or exertion.

جَرَتْ مَطَامِعِي مِنْ كَرَمِكَ عَلَى بُلُوغِ المُرَادِ مِنْ غَيْرِ اسْتِحْقَاقٍ مِنِّي وَلَا اسْتِعْدَادْ. أَسْأَلُكَ بِوَاحِدِ الآحَادِ وَمَشْهُودِ الأَشْهَادِ سَلَامَةَ مِنْحَةِ الوِدَادِ مِنْ مِحْنَةِ البِعَادِ وَمَحْوِ ظُلْمَةِ العِنَادِ بِنُورِ شَمْسِ الرَّشَادْ، وَفَتْحَ أَبْوَابِ السَّدَادِ بِأَيْدٍ مِدَادٍ إِنَّ اللهَ لَطِيفٌ بِالعِبَادْ.

jarat maṭāma ʿī min karamika ʿalā bulūghi-l-murādi min ghayri-stiḥqāqin minnī wa la-sti ʿdād. as ʾaluka bi-wāḥidi-l-āḥādi wa mashhūdi-l-ashhādi salāmata minḥati-l-widādi min miḥnati-l-bi ʿādi wa maḥwa ẓulmati-l- ʿinādi bi-nūri shamsi-r-rashād, wa fatḥa abwābi-s-sadādi bi-aydin midādin inna Allāha Laṭīfun bi-l- ʿibād.

My hopes overflow from Your Generosity to reach my desire, without any worth or preparation from me. I ask You, by the oneness of singularities and the witnessed of witnesses, the safe passage of the gift of love, through the tribulation of distance, and the erasure of the darkness of stubbornness, through the light of the sun of guidance, and the opening of the doors of felicity through the hands of providence. Indeed, Allah is Gentle with His servants.

رَبِّ إِنِّي أَسْأَلُكَ فَنَاءَ آنِيَّةِ وُجُودِي وَبَقَاءَ أُمْنِيَّةِ شُهُودِي، وَفِرَاقَ بَيْنِيَّةِ شَاهِدِي وَمَشْهُودِي بِجَمْعِ عَيْنِيَّةِ وُجُودِي بِمَوجُودِي. سَيِّدِي سَلِّمْ عُبُودِيَّتِي بِحَقِّكَ مِنْ عَمَاءِ وَهْمِ رُؤْيَةِ الأَغْيَارْ، وَأَلْحِقْ بِي كَلِمَتِكَ السَّابِقَةِ لِلْمُصْطَفَيْنَ الأَخْيَارْ،

Rabbi innī as ʾaluka fanā ʾa āniyyati wujūdī wa baqā ʾa umniyyati shuhūdī, wa firāqa bayniyyati shāhidī wa mashhūdī bi-jam ʿi ʿayniyyati wujūdī bi-mawjūdī. Sayyidī sallim ʿubūdiyyatī bi-ḥaqqika min ʿamā ʾi wahmi ru ʾiyati-l-aghiyār, wa alḥiq bī kalimatika-s-sābiqati li-l-muṣṭafayna-l-akhyār,

Oh, my Lord, I ask You the annihilation of the identity of my existence and subsistence of the hope of my witnessing, the departure of the distance between my witness and witnessed by gathering the essence of my being with what is found in me. Oh, my Master, save my servanthood, through Your Truth, from the blind illusion of perceiving others. Deliver, to me, Your Word that had already preceded to those chosen and elected.

وَاغْلِبْ عَلَى أَمْرِي بِاخْتِيَارِكَ فِي جَمِيعِ الأَوْطَارِ وَالأَطْوَارْ، وَانْصُرْنِي بِالتَّوْحِيدِ وَالاسْتِوَاءِ فِي الحَرَكَةِ وَالاسْتِقْرَارْ. حَبِيبِي أَسْأَلُكَ سَرِيعَ الوِصَالِ وَبَدِيعَ الجَمَالِ وَمَنِيعَ الجَلَالِ وَرَفِيعَ الكَمَالِ فِي كُلِّ حَالٍ وَمَآلْ، يَا مَنْ هُوَ هُوَ هُوَ يَا هُوَ يَا مَنْ لَيْسَ إِلَّا هُوْ،

wa-ghlib ʿalā amrī bi-khtiyārika fī jamīʿi-l-awṭāri wa-l-aṭwār, wa-nṣurnī bi-t-tawḥīdi wa-l-stiwāʾi fi-l-ḥarakati wa-l-istiqrār. Ḥabībī asʾaluka sarīʿa-l-wiṣāli wa badīʿa-l-jamāli wa manīʿa-l-jalāli wa rafiʿa-l-kamāli fī kulli ḥālin wa maʾāl, yā man Huwa yā Huwa yā man laysa illā Hū,

Overcome my affair, by your election, in all needs and conditions. Grant me victory, through oneness and steadiness, in movement and stillness. Oh, my Beloved, I ask You a swift union, splendid beauty, impervious majesty and lofty perfection in every state and return. Oh, You who is He, He, He, Oh He and none other than He.

أَسْأَلُكَ بِالغَيْبِ الأَطْلَسِ بِالعَيْنِ الأَقْدَسِ فِي اللَّيْلِ إِذَا عَسْعَسَ وَالصُّبْحِ إِذَا تَنَفَّسَ إِنَّهُ لَقَوْلُ رَسُولٍ كَرِيمٍ ذِي قُوَّةٍ عِنْدَ ذِي العَرْشِ مَكِينْ، مُطَاعٍ ثَمَّ أَمِينْ، بِلِسَانٍ عَرَبِيٍّ مُبِينْ، وَإِنَّهُ لَتَنْزِيلُ رَبِّ العَالَمِينْ، حُكْمَ مُحْكِمِ الأَمْرِ بِرَوحِهِ المُتَلَوِّنِ فِي صُنْعِ التَّبْيِينِ بِصِبَغِ التَّمْكِينْ.

as'aluka bi-l-ghaybi-l-aṭlasi bi-l-'ayni-l-aqdasi fi-l-layli idhā 'as'asa wa-ṣ-ṣubḥi idhā tanaffasa innahu la-qawlu rasūlin karīmin dhī quwwatin 'inda Dhi-l-'Arshi makīn, muṭā'in thamma amīn, bi-lisānin 'arabiyyin mubīn, wa innahu la-tanzīlu Rabbi-l-'ālamīn, ḥukma Muḥkimi-l-amri bi-rūḥihi-l-mutalawwini fī ṣun'i-t-tabiyīni bi-ṣibaghi-t-tamkīn.

I ask You, by the overarching silken unseen, by the Holiest Essence, in the night as it darkens and morning as it breathes, indeed, it is the utterance of a noble messenger, with power and ability in the court of the Owner of the Throne. He is obeyed therein and trustworthy, in an eloquent Arabic tongue. Indeed, it is cast from the Lord of the worlds, the ruling of the One who secured the affair, through His Ease that is colored in molds of clarification in dyes of ability.

وَأَسْأَلُكَ اللهُمَّ حَمْلَ ذَلِكَ لِذَاتِي عَلَى يَدِ نَسِيمِ حَيَاتِي بِأَرْوَاحِ تَحِيَّاتِي فِي صَلَوَاتِكَ الطَّيِّبَاتِ وَتَسْلِيمَاتِكَ الدَّائِمَاتِ عَلَى وَسِيلَةِ حُصُولِ المَطَالِبِ وَوَصْلَةِ وُصُولِ الحَبَائِبْ، وَعَلَى كُلِّ مَنْسُوبٍ إِلَيْهِ فِي كُلِّ المَرَاتِبِ إِلَى الحَقِّ المُبِينْ، وَاجْعَلْنَا مِنْ خَوَاصِّهِمْ آمِينْ.

I ask You, oh Allah, to carry all of that for my essence, upon the hand of my life's breeze, through the spirits of my greetings in Your Elegant Prayers and Continuous Salutations upon the mean for obtaining desires and connection for the arrival of loved ones, and upon all who are attributed to him ﷺ, in all ranks, to the Real and Most-Evident, and make us from among their elect, amen.

وَصَلَّى اللهُ عَلَى سَيِّدِنَا وَنَبِيِّنَا مُحَمَّدٍ وَعَلَى آلِهِ وَأَوْلَادِهِ، وَأَزْوَاجِهِ وَذُرِّيَاتِهِ وَأَتْبَاعِهِ وَأَصْحَابِهِ أَجْمَعِينْ، سُبْحَانَ رَبِّكَ رَبِّ العِزَّةِ عَمَّا يَصِفُونْ، وَسَلَامٌ عَلَى الْمُرْسَلِينْ، وَالحَمْدُ للهِ رَبِّ العَالَمِينْ.

wa ṣalla-Allāhu ʿalā sayyidinā wa nabiyyinā Muḥammadin wa ʿalā ālihi wa awlādih, wa azwājihi wa dhurriyātihi wa atbāʿihi wa aṣḥābihi ajmaʿīn, subḥāna Rabbika Rabbi-l-ʿIzzati ʿammā yaṣifūn, wa salāmun ʿala-l-mursalīn, wa-l-ḥamdu lillāhi Rabbi-l- ʿālamīn.

May Allah send His Prayers upon our master and prophet Muhammad ﷺ, his family, children, wives, descendants, followers, and companions entirely. May He be glorified, Your Lord the Lord of Exaltedness, above what they describe. Abundant salutations be upon the messengers and all praise is due to Allah, the Lord of the worlds.

تَمَّ بِحَمْدِ اللهِ

tamma bi-ḥamdi-Allāh

Completed, by the Grace of Allah

www.ingramcontent.com/pod-product-compliance
Lightning Source LLC
Chambersburg PA
CBHW041127110526
44592CB00020B/2716
9781938058677